BROKEN

*How Being Broken Unlocked the Greatest
Success of My Life*

Greg Yates

Broken: How Being Broken Unlocked the Greatest Success of My
Life

ISBN-10: 1517255023

ISBN-13: 978-1517255022

The story that is told in Broken *is one that needs to be told. It needs to be recounted, for it is a narrative that ends twice. The first ending seems to be one of closure, in that it brings a dark chapter in Mr. Yates' life to somewhat of an end, in which unknowing and sometimes driven choices eventually led him to federal prison. Yet there is an ending which is, in effect, still unfolding. There are new lessons that are continually being learned, conclusions are interpreted differently, actions are now observed and reflected upon for different outcomes. What Yates learned about living and processing his life, has glimpses of the best in any story of transformation.* Broken *is important reading for the insight it precipitates, for those who want to deliberately contemplate the trajectory of their life.*

Michael W. Benson, National Evangelist
The Priesthood Motorcycle Ministry

In Broken, *Greg Yates tells the story of his incredible journey from living the American Dream to landing in prison. Valedictorian, multi-millionaire, devoted family man, philanthropist, devout Christian-- he thought he was doing everything God wanted him to do. Until the Feds raided his business and seized everything. In his brilliant three-tiered narrative, Yates reveals how it all went down, weaving in both his deepest intuitions about what was happening to him at the time and his raw, primal conversations with God while in prison. The result is a brutally honest story of redemption and a practical guide for letting God transform our broken past into our greatest breakthrough.*

Jaymie Simmon, author of The God Gene

Broken *is an epic true life story of huge proportion that leads the reader down a path of triumph, hardship, resilience, and ultimately to peace. Greg Yates reveals truth in his thinking process and feelings rarely spoken in Christian circles. The depth of Grace is an overriding theme and ever-present.* Broken *is a journey. And we identify with it, walk it, feel it and actually experience it along with Yates. It is rare that a written work can be so revealing and profound on a personal level. How do we forgive others? How do we forgive ourselves? Experience this journey as forgiveness is revealed as only God can reveal it when we are "broken." Amazing!*

John R. Nimmo, John Maxwell Certified Speaker and Coach Southern Development, LLC

Broken *is a powerful book. Almost everyone in the market place, especially those in leadership positions, will identify with parts (hard work, financial rewards, recognition, generosity, pride, etc.) of Greg's journey. When we are successful, we often think: "God is blessing us, so we must be doing things right." In the well known 23rd Psalm, God's word tells us: "He makes us lie down in green pastures." When we go through the process of making and breaking to lie down, it is not pleasant and we do not see the green pastures; it is after we are broken and have surrendered that we see it. That is when the miracle happens; when we find out we are truly blessed (not just in material things) and are thankful for the process. (1 Thes. 5:8)*
This book is a must read! You will be blessed.

Albert Diepeveen, Former Chairman of CBMC International

Yates has given a very honest and sobering assessment of business; a very detailed account of doing business in America that is then caught in the cross hairs of the government. A riveting account of rising to business success, falling to business disaster, and then experiencing restoration.

Carl Boender, Legacy Leadership Forums

Yates' transparent telling of his personal journey describes how his God-given passion for excellence developed beyond his relationship with his "Father." The result took Yates somewhere he never planned to go. Yates weaves his past and present throughout Broken *while seeking the true heart of God. I have benefitted from* Broken *because I resonate with Yates' passion and his heart for communion with his Lord. I will read* Broken *again for the purpose of soaking in its truth. It is an "iron sharpening iron" experience.*

Tony Fightmaster, Director of Church and University Relations at Olivet Nazarene University

Yates is a powerful communicator, but that's not what makes this book so powerful. It's the raw transparency and honesty that is poured into these pages. The story of God showing His strength through the humility, emptiness, and brokenness of his chosen vessel. Compelling, touching, and at times gut-wrenching... a real story of redemption.

Bill DeWees, Voice Over Talent
Bill DeWees Media Inc.

Table of Contents

BROKEN

How Being Broken Unlocked the Greatest
Success of My Life

Greg Yates

Why Read This Book

If your heart is broken, you'll find God right there; if you're kicked in the gut, He'll help you catch your breath. (The Message, Psalm 34:18)

When you picked up my book today, it wasn't by accident. God is trying to get your attention. It's what He does. He's been trying to get your attention your entire life, just like He did with me.

I've experienced wealth and success. I've also experienced prison and a near fatal car crash. God used every minute of it to get my attention. That's all He ever wanted.

Getting my attention took longer than it should have. I had to be broken in order to understand how brokenness brings life without limitations. Now, brokenness has become my way of life, overwriting my limiting beliefs daily, unlocking my greatest success.

If the feverish pursuit of success is the defining characteristic of your life, you'll understand this book.

I fought to remain unbroken! I kicked and screamed to maintain my false reality of self-made success. My explosive, raw and bloody battle with the government taught me more about myself, and about God's presence, than success ever did.

Why Should You Read This Book?

My story is proof it's never too late. When I was at my worst,

God gave me a freedom and a peace through brokenness. I just wanted to share my story, but once I wrote it down I saw four distinct phases of brokenness:

1. Unmasking a Broken Heart

My broken heart was masked by extreme self-reliance. Here, I share the raw vulnerability of my compulsive behavior, hoping it will help you avoid my mistakes.

2. Detecting Brokenness

Maybe you're fiercely defending your feelings of isolation or your struggling relationships. Perhaps you're in denial about financial questions or deadlines with no answers. This book came to you just in time. *Early detection* is the most important thing I can share with you about brokenness. Don't learn the way I did (the hard way).

3. Embracing Brokenness

If you're trying to survive a crisis, this book can help you embrace brokenness to experience your breakthrough.

4. Praying To Be Used Through Brokenness

This book is bathed in prayer that God would embed His message for you into it. God has a fresh encounter in store for you, perhaps through the 'thrill' of brokenness. Brokenness may be your path to Breakthrough.

This Is Your Chance

Brokenness is a radical topic. Nobody wants to believe it, but eventually we all face it. Whether through loss, financial disaster or just the pain of mediocrity, being broken will give you the unexpected chance of a lifetime.

The Raw Truth About My Story

I was broken so I could become all I was created to be. It was brutal, it was painful, and it was the path of brokenness required for this passionate, determined, stubborn man to be radically changed.

Here's how it happened…

Confessions of the Author

On a hot day in July of 2011, my world was completely ripped apart when our parking lot was invaded by armed federal officers. It felt like the first time in my life when I was NOT in control. A truckload of documents was confiscated and the knife of accusation was buried deep into my chest. Everything I placed confidence in was ripped away. The root of my empowering beliefs was uncovered for everyone to see. The steps toward my complete renewal had begun. I would pass through the fires of hell before purification could be complete.

How did my storybook life explode into a tabloid nightmare? How could my best intentions be defined as criminal? When did my compass stop pointing north, or did it? When did the demands of success become more than I could fulfill?

Have you ever come face-to-face with a nuclear meltdown in your life that couldn't be stopped? Something that couldn't be wished away, refused or covered with avoidance and denial?

Have you ever screamed at God in disbelief because He was allowing your life to fall apart? I did. I fought to prevent the destruction of my own identity. I believed that God's nature in me was real, and I was empowered by my beliefs.

With all of your hard work to please God, have you ever felt He didn't even notice? I was living out the parable of the talents, earning and performing for the master so I could gain His approval. I acknowledged that God was the one who blessed it all. How could

I be reduced to accusation and innuendo when I had constructed perfectly logical explanations for every decision?

I believed the power of the human spirit was the ultimate proof of God's favor. I believed in myself. I was the underdog who overcame every obstacle through sheer force of will. God's blessings were all the proof I needed that He was pleased with me. Until now.

Have you read the book or watched the movie about Louie Zamperini? The title is *Unbroken*. He was shot down, survived a month on a life raft near starvation, and was almost beaten to death again and again in a Japanese POW camp during World War II. In his spare time, he managed to save lives and humiliate the enemy with defiant endurance. I love that story. Isn't that what we were built for? Isn't that the definition of success?

I believed in that pattern of thinking. I would have persisted in it forever if I'd been given the choice. I had no lack of belief, confidence or good intent, but I watched that movie while I was serving a sentence for bank fraud in federal prison.

This is my story. I hope my story helps you to never go through this. If you're looking for platitudes and wise instruction about how I 'got it right,' you picked up the wrong book. I'm the poster boy for living fast and furious; lots of action, but sooner or later there is going to be a fiery crash. This is a story of hard work and success beyond my wildest dreams. This is a story of pain and deception, filled with false assumptions on my part. This is also the story of my pathway to truth, even though my internal beliefs weren't going to let me go there without a fight.

Mine is not a story of conformity, but of volatility and a thirst for risk; a story in which God himself became my adversary. He personally took charge of the demolition and the restoration of my life.

Do you know what it feels like to have someone say you need to change? An intervention? Well, I didn't need God to save me from my life. I was just fine.

The walls I built and trusted are the tragedy of this story. The identity I relied on was efficiently wrapped in self-affirming layers. I thought this would protect me from any attack. I couldn't accept that all my good intentions were meaningless. I wasn't done fighting. I wasn't ready to surrender; as long as I could lift my arms, I would fight. Isn't that the true spirit of being 'unbroken'?

The questions addressed in this book are as a result of the desperate cries of my brokenness and the resulting stories of my life. Maybe you can relate. Have you ever wondered…

- Is your confidence really in God, or in the manifestation of His blessings in your life?

- Do the driving beliefs of your life put you at risk for failure (perhaps explosive failure)?

- Is your desire for self-sufficiency really just because of enormous self-pride?

- Is there still significance for your life after complete failure and brokenness?

- Are you completely disqualified for use in business or the church if you have failed?

- Is your life worth living if you've blown up the things, and hurt the people, that matter most?

- Is it possible to redeem yourself?

Once it happened to me, the yellow brick road was gone. The fear of the unknown came masked in horrors I had never imagined. I hungered to find the 'unbroken' path again, on the other side of this monstrous event. Isn't that what we all hope for?

What I discovered was the revolutionary force that liberated my entire existence. Instead of freedom through being unbroken, my brokenness abolished the powerful, limiting beliefs at the cellular level of my life. To be free of these cancerous beliefs in their advanced stages required radical intervention.

In this book, I candidly share my experiences—both unimaginable and humorous. I wrote endlessly by hand whilst in prison. I'm sharing many of those personal bombshells with you. Please be warned: these are my raw, unedited thoughts as the flood of emotions and despair poured out of me toward God.

What if your own conflicting beliefs forced you into submission? What if you faced public humiliation, financial ruin and federal incarceration while your family clung to each other for survival?

Walk with me as I share the lessons I've learned. Identify the false and limiting beliefs that magnify the distortion of biblical truth. Uncover the false assumptions buried in you before they dictate your fate.

I can now share these breakthrough lessons with you because I was completely *Broken*.

Have you ever truly admitted to the voices in your head? Even when they're egotistical and completely unacceptable? How much influence does self-talk really have? Who is really in control? What do we really believe?

Chapter One: Confronting My Beliefs

Boardrooms were familiar and comfortable, but this padded church pew felt like the most awkward place I'd ever been. Heat seemed to radiate from my collar in the silence of a thousand piercing eyes. My typical defenses didn't work as I fidgeted, adjusting my legs and looking for a comfortable position. My eyes diverted to Vicki, who seemed more radiant than I had seen her in recent days. How could she feel so relaxed in this place? It was the most stressful time of the week for me; a set-aside from the flurry of business, yes, but stress I did *not* need. Why was I so uncomfortable with these people? Why did I feel so out of place? I didn't know, but I trusted my instincts. Why couldn't I just worship God in my own way, in my own comfortable surroundings?

Suddenly I remembered my school days when the teacher seemed to intentionally 'dumb down' the material so everyone could understand. I was bored. I was tired of over-simplified theories. I wanted something challenging, and wasn't that what made me special? Wasn't that what made me successful?

Vicki and I had always been 'right' for each other. We had always found our own sidebar of fun, no matter where we were or how tedious the situation. She repeatedly saved me when I was trapped by conversations with people who wanted to have a piece of me. We had a code, of sorts. She read me like a book after our 30 plus years of marriage. So many of our friends had tumbled from marriage to marriage, but we had stuck it out. Sure, we had rough patches, but for some reason the thought of being apart seemed like failure to me and I always found my way home again, even when it seemed hopeless. We both knew we were better together than we were apart. Perspective had changed over the years, but love was still undeniable. Vicki made me feel more successful than even my balance sheet or businesses. Most of the time, anyway.

I wondered if our pastor ever really worked an actual job. Could he understand the stress of having so many people employed and depending on him? In fact, I wondered suddenly if he even knew how to balance his own checkbook, yet he never seemed shy about asking for money. Asking for the order... *I guess I can respect that*, I thought as I occupied my mind with random thoughts. I suppose that makes sense. The pastor was really a salesman, never really in tune with what it takes to run the business or do the actual 'work.' He's the guy who builds relationships so he can make sales.

The parallel had credibility to me, and the roles of 'church' began to fall into place. I could see that it was a business, even if often poorly run. I didn't like the feeling of being a follower. I certainly wasn't a satisfied customer, yet I believed in God and that seemed like the only constant. God was upper management and I was tired of dealing with mid-level managers.

I imagined I was going to a department meeting rather than meeting with the boss. I didn't like it. I didn't appreciate being spoken to like one of the sheep. I wasn't the guy whose emotions indulged in 'warm and fuzzy' feelings. My stare continued to penetrate Pastor Phil as he labored on.

Categorizing people was a strength I took pride in. Once I had someone pegged, I wasn't surprised any longer. I could hold them up like a glass of water and look right through them. I knew Pastor Phil. I had seen his sincerity, and yet I had also seen him perform for his audience. He had a job to get paid for, and this one looked pretty cushy from my point of view.

Vicki squeezed my hand as we stood for the benediction, which jolted me back to reality. The uneasy feeling subsided as I turned to Paul and Joyce, sitting behind us in the sanctuary. I admired Paul, even though I didn't know him that well. His relaxed ease was always present. I wondered if Paul simply had a stress-free job or if he didn't know everything I knew about life. What a burden. Sundays seemed the worst. All the details crashing in for the coming week. The quiet left me alone with my thoughts and it was torture, not peaceful worship. Perhaps someone else was worrying about Paul's job like I worried about the employees on my $275,000/week payroll.

I knew there was a God and I knew we had a special relationship. We took care of each other. I stood up for Him and made sure people knew I was a Christian every chance I got. People even apologized if they swore around me. After all, God had clearly blessed me with a unique intellect and a wonderful family. God gave me talents and I was determined not to let God down. Pastor Phil was busy laying out everything God expects of us, but I already knew exactly what God expected of me. I had the gift of making money and I gave my part to the church. God expected me to work hard. Anything short of that would disappoint God, which would never be acceptable to me. Yes, God was good to me but I knew what God wanted in return. I was proud of the endless effort I put into proving that God was not wrong about me.

I did enjoy the social time after the service. Walking through the church on my way toward the door, I could feel the energy. Each step, smiling as people acknowledged and embraced me with clear respect and admiration. I enjoyed the social aspect of church, just like any other social event. After all, I had proven myself on the field of battle and many of the people there that day were supporting their families thanks to my business, and they knew it. The church probably couldn't survive if I weren't regularly contributing.

I felt my shoulders spread as I looked over the fine trappings of the facility. It was a great place for people to come together. My own family really benefited from this place. It was a good feeling. Yes, partially a burden, but a certain satisfaction as well. Other people didn't have the capacity to comprehend my world, but they did know this: I was a good guy. For today, that was enough.

"Thank you, God, that I am not like other men. You have given me a comprehension of life unlike the dullness others live in. You have blessed me and I am here to publicly acknowledge that I am one of your followers. Amen."

The entire dialogue sounds a bit harsh to admit, doesn't it? Arrogant and self-obsessed, to say the least. When I read it now I want to laugh, but I've let a number of Christian businessmen read it and they admit they have felt the same way.

Sharing hidden thoughts isn't easy. Until recently, I never admitted them to myself. Laugh with me about some of my circumstantial beliefs, but realize that much of it is an unspoken mirror into your own life. Listen as I dialogue back and forth, making assumptions and allowing my (often false) beliefs to manifest into action.

My Circumstantial Beliefs

I loved God. The circumstances of my life led to a defined set of beliefs that I never questioned. I call them circumstantial beliefs; the beliefs that 'seem' to be foregone conclusions, seem consistent with what you have experienced your entire life—beliefs that could be good or bad.

Of course God loved me. Of course He approved of me. Look at the blessings He has given me, at the responsibility. He has placed hundreds of people in my care. The Bible says if I am faithful in these few things, He will give me even more.

The blessings were actually a heavy burden. Knowing the expectation was high kept me focused and alone. The weight imposed by my circumstantial beliefs ran my life. From the start, the conflict was building. The approval was essential, especially from God.

Do you ever feel trapped and alone when everyone has big expectations of you? Do you unconsciously reject that kind of pressure or feel manipulated?

I hated the quiet. The thoughts were so random, so illogical, I couldn't imagine how to contain them. The voices in my head were locked in fierce battle, but as long as I kept things fast and furious, everything seemed fine. I kept my endorphins and adrenaline pumping. I felt praise and respect. I lived a life of power with a clear confidence in the sheer force of my will. I knew I could change the room just by being in it.

My self-esteem was alive with desire for the approval of others. I could smell the aphrodisiac of it all. There was no reason to stop. I didn't need the money; I thrived on the affirmation. In the grand course of life, I was valuable to others. I was needed, and I needed to be needed.

Does the thrill of the 'deal' create an addictive compulsion in your life? Have you ever felt euphoria in the power of your own signature controlling a contract? I have. I wanted everyone to know I had arrived; I was one of the 'big boys.' When opportunity came knocking, I had a hunger for more.

I craved knowledge. I was hungry to understand what propelled others to success. Still, in every quiet moment, a haunting question pounded in my head as I entered my 50s. Have you heard it? The question that refuses to be satisfied by more laps around the proverbial track of life? The question that returns no matter how fast you prove you can go? "Am I the man I was created to be?"

It was a nagging question and it drove me wild, seeking more of everything I already had. The question irritated me, provoked me and choked me out when I least expected it. Maybe it was a calling or maybe the ancient question planted in all of us from the beginning. Whatever the case, it was a question I could not answer. The anger of it unraveled any peace I found. I didn't need God to change me or save me from anything. I was just fine. The addiction of my life had needs but I was *not* out of control.

Isn't there an addictive strength in the significance of work? It drove the self-image I depended on. I didn't see the co-dependency of it. The work needed me and I needed the work. I knew God had blessed me. I wasn't perfect, but I was pursuing what I believed I was destined for. The circumstances of my life came together in a powerful representation of the man I had become. I was convinced God was on my side and had gifted me with indestructible success.

Have you ever been so convinced about who you are that you never considered where the evidence came from? Have you ever felt powerful conflict when something or someone tried to challenge your beliefs?

I was fine with the beliefs I had about myself. I was on the far end of the spectrum, far from anything I thought was limiting me or holding me back. The continuity of my life from past to future was already fixed. I refused to linger in the quiet where the nagging question pulled at me in its pointless and illogical way.

I never doubted the man I had become. My beliefs, even if circumstantial, had fixed my destiny. They powered my fate from the obscurity of my subconscious. I accepted them as truth, until I was broken.

I can't help but note, even in the greatest question of my life the framing of it exists around the word "I." What "I" should be, should do, should become. It's impossible to write about this era of my life without an exaggerated and egocentric expression of the word "I." Until my brokenness led to breakthrough, I didn't even see it.

Chapter Two: The Blessing Phenomenon

I walked into Jerry's house after school, looking forward to a bottle of RC cola he'd promised. Our bikes out front, we were heading to the vacant lot across from school to play some ball. Jerry wasn't much of a ball player, but he was fun to hang out with. He did whatever I wanted to do.

Jerry, for reasons I didn't understand at the time, hadn't invited me to spend time at his house. Then, the first and only time I went to Jerry's house, it surprised me to see Jerry's dad sitting on the sofa watching TV. My dad always seemed to be at work. Soon I found out something about life I had never imagined in my nine short years.

As we approached the refrigerator, I was startled when Jerry's dad suddenly yelled. Swearing and screaming at us, he jumped up revealing that he was wearing only his underwear. Pointing with a beer bottle, he came angrily toward us. Jerry looked at me with horror in his eyes, then ran toward the back door. Instinctively, I followed. We ran until we could no longer hear the yelling, then we ran another block just to be sure.

What had happened? Jerry didn't want to talk about it. We snuck back for our bikes and I hurriedly headed home. It had never occurred to me that anyone lived differently from my own family, let alone that our dynamic was rare. I didn't know I was rich; rich in the wonderful role models and unconditional love of my parents.

I was given the perfect launch pad. I hear people blame their limitations on their parents, but that wasn't true for me. I had a clear road to cruise with minimal baggage. I was nurtured with the affirmations of loving parents. I was given the belief that I was something very special. That belief was circumstantial of course, because I had been blessed.

I learned the value of a strong work ethic from my father. He worked long hours as a tool maker. He was a rock I could always count on. His expectations were high and his standards were clear. I never doubted his desires for our conduct or his resolve in enforcing the rules. I also never doubted his love.

Sometimes when he worked all night on a rush job, he let me come. I slept in the back of a truck from which I could watch. I could get a coke from the fridge in the boss' office for ten cents. I can close my eyes and go back there now. I smell cutting oil and feel secure confidence. My dad was the one they called when the heat was on. I was proud. It was another circumstance to support my growing beliefs.

My mother was also a trailblazer. She grew up with dyslexia and poor eyesight in a time when it was not diagnosed. She taught herself to play the piano by 'ear' because she couldn't read the notes. She went to Olivet Nazarene College to study for the ministry. While many believed it wasn't the 'place' for a woman, perhaps even unbiblical, she knew what God had demanded of her. She would not relent. She graduated in six years and gave birth to three children. We were poor, but I thrived on her indomitable belief. Another block was laid in the foundation of my self-image.

I had a perfect grade point average in high school and was co-valedictorian of my graduating class. I remember as a young boy hearing my parents talk about how smart I was. I decided I would never get anything less than an A, no matter what it took. Living up to expectations was my norm. I believed there was nothing I couldn't accomplish if I wanted it badly enough.

The foundational belief in my ability to perform never lacked confidence or self-assurance. If anyone could do it, so could I. My foundation was built on the praise and acceptance of others. As I got older, I needed more of it. It was the single thing that propelled me to success. Performance was the cornerstone for my foundational belief.

Of course, I gave God credit for that. I'm not a heathen. Let's see; God created me and gave me talents. He rewards me for using them. That makes me acceptable to him, right? I loved my life and people loved me. What could be better? My circumstantial beliefs had found evidence to support them. Now it was time to attack my goals with a vengeance.

Have you ever wondered if your blessings were your greatest strength or possibly your greatest weakness? I call this the blessing phenomenon. Like so many things in my life, I accepted blessings as evidence that I could depend on my own performance to please God and achieve the goals of my life.

Beliefs Reinforced by Love

I headed toward college, full of hubris. The world seemed an endless opportunity to prove myself.

One day after a workout, I was in the library studying for a test. Out of the corner of my eye, I noticed someone moving around my table. I looked up to see a cute blonde shaking her head as she gave me the once-over. I had seen her around campus but didn't know her name. I even remembered seeing her smile at me once in the cafeteria. What a beautiful smile. I looked away, but now she boldly paced around my table, gazing at me with purpose.

Have you ever asked yourself, "is this really happening to me?" I have, and I definitely did at that unforeseen moment. She shook her head as she walked.

"I think you need to work on your lats a little more," she muttered. "You look a little lean in the lats." Suddenly she grinned and jetted away.

I hadn't said a word. I wondered what had just happened. A relationship with so much power and passion had been born in that moment. 36 years later, I vividly remember that night with the grin of a schoolboy.

Isn't it crazy how many things we incorporate into our beliefs? They create momentum before we even realize how powerful they are. Vicki brought even more support to my growing foundational beliefs. God was good to me. He must need me to accomplish something that only I can accomplish.

After my sophomore year in college, Vicki and I decided to get married. At the time, I thought I was mature. I had all the answers to life, but I was only 20 years old. Vicki was 19. All of our friends thought we were crazy, especially because we were still in school. We were in love. I realize now what a tightrope we were walking. At the time, we couldn't be dissuaded.

I used to have a sign that hung on the front of my TV, which said: "Have you accomplished your goals today?" This was before the remote control. If you wanted to watch TV, you had to physically turn it on. If I was going to turn it on, I had to move that sign. I was determined to have the big house and nice cars; to be satisfied and to live happily ever after.

The Blessing Phenomenon of my life led me to the conclusion that I was destined for unlimited wealth and success. It never occurred to me that wealth and success in business would not include peace, satisfaction and contentment. I had chosen a target; I defined success as I believed it to be. I launched myself into a life of relentless obsession to achieve it.

They say you should dig your well before you're thirsty. They never say anything about the fox holes or the bomb shelters you're going to need. I had achieved liftoff but I had no idea what it was going to cost me to break through the atmosphere. As young men, we all dream dreams. Have your dreams included the details and course corrections you need? Mine, clearly, did not. I was loaded on a rocket ship with high-octane fuel. It never occurred to me it was potentially a very large bomb.

Have you ever wondered where and when your path shifted? As I share the evaluation of my own beliefs, brokenness and breakthrough, story after story comes to mind. They are the circumstances, compiling the unconscious beliefs which anchored me.

I'd love to jump to the end, to tell you what I've discovered, but these are the building blocks that made me and sabotaged me. You must see my past to share my breakthrough.

Chapter Three: The Birth of Conflicting Beliefs

My head pounded as if a blood vessel had exploded behind my right temple. A cold sensation traveled to my jaw as my right side lost function. What was happening to me? I was 36 years old and physically strong. I worked long days and had never experienced anything more than the flu.

I shifted my weight onto my right leg and it didn't move. Catching myself awkwardly, I avoided falling to the concrete floor. I realized this was more than a migraine. I didn't have time for this. I could not be weak and I could not be sick. Three shifts a day, 6 days a week, I was in demand. Production was critical to meet our customers' needs. Nearly 400 people relied on my scheduling and waited for my approval before taking action in their day.

Terry, around 15 at the time, was to my left. We were late for an evening trip with the family for shopping and dinner. Doug was to my right, having tracked me down in a sprint from the press department at almost 7pm. Time stood still as I came to grips with this near collapse.

Doug waited for the answer to a question I hadn't heard. The ringing in my ear locked my consciousness. I wondered if the lights were going out. Gripping a chair, I managed to look desperately to Terry, who immediately grabbed my arm.

I apologized, said I wasn't feeling well, and began hobbling toward the door. Terry and Doug were alongside, supporting me. I learned later that my condition was very obvious to them. I climbed into the Tahoe and asked Vicki to drive as I assessed my status. It occurred to me that something might really be wrong with me, but my ego could not indulge the idea. I remembered hearing that most men who die from heart attacks or strokes refuse to believe they're having them. I don't remember how we got there, but soon we were in the emergency room.

For years, my typical work day began around 5am and extended to 6 or 7pm. Phone calls littered the evening, often until 3am. This was my identity. This was the demand placed on my life which validated the beliefs I held. I believed nothing could happen without me. If we took a vacation, it was because a natural gap in production seemed to appear. I would call Vicki to make some last minute plans for immediate departure. This was my life. I would never have admitted how proud I was to be so busy. Even if self-induced, the demand of business affirmed my identity. It seemed real and it concealed any cracks in my foundational beliefs.

As the tests progressed in the E.R., I felt helpless. I had experienced a TIA, what they called a 'mini-stroke.' It could have been much worse. I was strongly cautioned about taking some time off and reducing my stress level. Life or death didn't really compute with me. There was no way I was going to slow down.

As a precaution, I went to Mayo Clinic for a complete physical. That week was one of the nicest vacations Vicki and I had for a while. It was just the two of us. We drove the ten hour trip and by the time it was over, I was incredibly relaxed. The doctors said I was in perfect health but my stress level was off the charts, which was starting to show some serious impacts on my body. I needed to reduce the stress in my life.

As we drove home, I considered my options. Perhaps if we bought a hot tub I could relax in it every night and still maintain the workload required of me. So, a hot tub was purchased and I was back to work.

The Random Development of Powerful Beliefs

What happened to my solid foundational beliefs? You know, the foundation that was supposed to support me for a lifetime? Were they supporting me, or was I supporting them?

How did I move from a solid foundation of beliefs to an emergency room where those beliefs were killing me?

The progression from marriage to retirement seems like a blur when you look back. I recall the process as a memorable and exciting dash from one stage to the next. Each step left me searching for the moment I would arrive at true satisfaction. It would no doubt be accompanied by financial independence and power. There is a problem, however, with living a life in pursuit of something you have not attained: you don't know what it's like, or even when you have it.

I had learned to ride a bike, water ski, even fly an airplane. I knew at any moment I could get back on that bike and ride it. I had confidence in what I had already experienced, but I had none of the ultimate satisfaction I was striving for. What did it look like? What did it feel like? I had no idea.

I remember the early days of our married life. I was far too consumed with the future to enjoy the present. Attending school, living off campus, trying to work and being too proud to accept help from our parents... it made our lives challenging. We were in love, carving out our future together so we could enjoy wealth and satisfaction when it came.

And then it happened. "We" were pregnant. The Corvette wouldn't hold a car seat. The finances couldn't support school along with a few hundred a month in diapers. Everything changed.

With six credit hours to go, I dropped out of school. It was necessary. I would finish later, when things were better financially. I rationalized that a degree wasn't going to control my future because nothing could hold me back. Unfortunately, I never finished. I later served on the Board of Trustees for that very school, but I never completed my degree.

I remember standing in our driveway with my brother, Jim. With his boot firmly on the rear bumper of my car, we talked about working together. We were brothers and had our share of bumpy roads and steely egos. Jim said something that night I can still hear vividly in the anchor of my soul. I still visualize the moment he said it. I can see the crack in the concrete that angled from the expansion joint to the grass. There were thousands of words spoken, but everything hinged on this single phrase: "Greg, I know we are better together than we can be apart."

Two Decades of Massive Momentum

The deal was done. The vision was cast. I had read the book *Acres of Diamonds*, but I never expected to live it. I was returning home to build on the foundation of the family business.

Have you experienced those moments when far more actually occurs than you realize? Moments that change our destiny, that impact who we become, who we meet, who we influence and who we hurt?

Our dad trained us from the time we were boys in the machinist trade. We worked summers and after school to make money. We escaped to college never intending to have a career in that field. How could I have imagined that little machine shop held such a powerful engine for growth; a business that within ten years would grow to more than fifty times its size in employees and in revenue?

34

For the next two decades, we poured ourselves into business and church. Both were blessed abundantly. A large percentage of the people we worked with also attended our church. We were the bosses at work, and almost by default we were key voices at church. Natural leaders get accustomed to being in charge. I was far too young to realize the pitfalls.

If it was happening, I was in the middle of it. If you needed help, I could give it. If you needed a job, you talked to me. If you needed an opinion on any subject, just give me a call. The momentum of my own presumption was still contained, but it was growing rapidly. I only knew that life was good and I had all of the money and attention I could ask for. I never questioned the premises of my life because they had resulted in money and power. I was sure peace and satisfaction were just around the corner.

Early Warning Signs

Our wives referred to themselves as shop-widows. Our plant was running three shifts a day, six days a week. The department heads answered to me. If there was an issue at 2 or 3am, they had strict instructions to call. Timing was critical to maintaining a JIT (Just in Time) product flow. We prided ourselves in being the highest quality, lowest cost lighting manufacturer in the country. If we were going to keep that production in the U.S., we had to prove it every day.

We built the tooling to make the products. Injection molds, stamping and deep draw dies, transfer press tooling. We designed and built secondary operations presses and one-of-a-kind automation. We created cellular operations which amplified our efficiency. We produced the parts. We had injection molders, transfer presses, deep draw and stamping presses, metal spinning and roll forming machines and a fabrication department. If that wasn't enough, we also powder-coated and assembled the products, and packaged them and shipped them to the customer's distribution centers. We maintained control over the entire process. If there was a bottleneck, it impacted the forecasting of the entire facility. Ultimately, whether it was valid or not, I carried that weight with me always.

That's where the conflicts began. Beliefs should empower you, not require you to be their slave. When you accept your foundational beliefs as truth, you begin to repeat the same things. I still believed I would eventually get the desired result. I never questioned the foundation of my beliefs. I thought the problem must lie in me.

Have you ever found yourself in complete denial when something challenges the assumptions or decisions you've made? Do you defend them instinctively? Does it even occur to you that you should question the underlying assumptions?

Laying in a CT scanner has a way of getting your attention. It was my first 'near nuclear' warning sign. I dismissed it. Anything that conflicted with my belief system was wrong. Sometimes you have to push through the pain. Obstacles define us. When the going gets tough, the tough get going.

My definition of sacrifice meant that anything in the way of my success or my work ethic had to be sacrificed. Anything and anyone. I was on a mission and nothing could stand in my way.

Chapter Four: Driven to Isolation

The potent floral arrangements were the only thing alive in my senses. I stood by the casket waiting for my turn to walk those last few agonizing steps. It seemed they were uphill and gravity was more than I could overcome. My heart was racing as I squeezed Vicki's hand for support. She had no idea what I knew. She was unprepared for the anger I anticipated.

Attending the funeral of a friend is one of the most difficult things you ever do. You've been there, haven't you? It's a numb feeling when you wonder why you are alive. You picture yourself in the casket while you stand in line to pay your respects. The tears have all been cried.

What if everyone attending the funeral believed you were responsible for the death? How would you deal with that? Even I believed I was responsible.

How did I get to this place? As our business grew, our employees became close friends. We were like family. Simultaneously, an overload of policies seemed required as our numbers grew into the hundreds. Our human resources director, along with insurance companies and lawyers, required we consider liability issues. Policies like drug testing and sexual harassment seemed necessary to protect ourselves. It all seemed logical.

Eventually, our changing view of the workplace intersected with our family-like employee experience. Relationships became a quantified series of documents. We spent more time explaining than embracing. I needed a mentor in these areas but I had none.

A knock at my door came with the disturbing news. One of my friends and fellow church members came back with a positive drug test. In that moment, I was face-to-face with the reality of law vs. grace. A piece of paper and a very logical procedure had been placed between me and someone I genuinely cared for. The theoretical beliefs I had about the 'people' side of the business had become a crisis of unprecedented proportion.

Later, we modified the policy to make provision for second chances and rehab. At the time, the only possibility was termination. We struggled to find another option. If we didn't follow our own policies, it would open us up to liability and possible law suits.

After many tears and conversations, we terminated him. I knew it would be difficult for him and his family. Legally, we couldn't disclose to anyone else the reason for his termination. I loved him on a personal level. He was good at his job, but 'policy' had dictated a path nobody wanted.

I justified the termination emotionally. He had known the policy and violated it. But at the funeral, that didn't help much as I tried to console his widow. He had found another job and was killed on that job in the first month. I blamed myself, and I wasn't alone in that. All I could do was further isolate myself.

At times, the burden of so many people depending on me was overwhelming. I started to cycle in and out of energy. I couldn't recover quickly enough. I started looking for anything that would provide a few moments of peace or satisfaction. I drank coffee by the gallons. I worked out. I distracted myself in any way I possibly could to find some new 'channel' to exploit.

I worked, worshipped and went to every event with the same people. Our children played with their children. Yet, I was isolated. I began to distrust friendships and imagine that every attempt was disingenuous.

It seemed that everyone wanted something of me. I became more and more guarded; more and more removed. Everything seemed part of a larger scheme that I couldn't quite get my arms around.

My foundational beliefs had become territorial. They had produced conflict and now they required segregation. The greater the resistance, the more I built walls to protect myself. The foundation of my life was fractured.

Retirement

Two years later, I sold my share of the business and retired. I was 38 and money was not an issue. I wanted to learn to play golf, but my friends were skeptical. It seems that golf is a relaxed sport and they weren't certain it was a good fit for me.

I bought the equipment and machine gunned thousands of balls into the field in front of our home. Vicki even mowed landing zones and mock Tee boxes. I read every book I could get my hands on. This was not something to be enjoyed, it was something to be conquered.

My golf game did improve, but I became bored with life. I was certain satisfaction would find me once I was freed from the demands of business. It never did. I came to realize that I needed to be needed. I needed to be busy. I began taking on consulting jobs. I worked internationally and had a great deal of experience in finance. It was a combination I hadn't planned, but there were very few conversations I wasn't prepared to have.

Ahhh, the speed of business again. The power of it. Those were my strengths and I didn't believe I was good at anything else. Making money and making deals were my comfort zone. They were my placebo for fulfillment. I never imagined how deep that vein could go.

I didn't have a clear landing zone but one thing was certain: I wasn't happy unless I was involved in passionate pursuit.

Chapter Five: The Bullet-Proof Nature of Compulsive Beliefs

I've never particularly enjoyed formal events or formal attire. I tend to be a jeans and T-shirt guy with boots and a Harley. Today was an overwhelming exception. Have you ever been asked to be the best man at someone's wedding? I could not have been more proud or humbled to get the call.

He was younger than me, but loved to talk and learn about stock trading and economics. We paper traded the markets for fun and talked business strategy for hours. In high school, he built an inventory tracking and time management system for our business. He even trained the employees. I was never very good with kids, but this one was different. He didn't need to be played with. He was an information sponge like me. He was hungry for the things that set us apart from everyone else.

When he was a senior in high school, I remember giving him a proud hug as he came off the football field. It wasn't planned, it just happened. I can still feel the sweat on his jersey and his wet hair against my head. Now, unbelievably, I was going to be his best man, and also the father of the groom.

What is it about those moments that make us feel bigger than life? What catalyzes the response which temporarily fills the void, anchors our emotions and boosts our self-esteem? Why doesn't it last?

A powerful belief system, even if inaccurate, has measurable consequences. Belief has actionable momentum like nothing else.

My beliefs were primarily designed by circumstances I had chosen to accept. It never occurred to me I should consciously prune those beliefs to meet a very specific standard.

When I was young, my mother and grandmother repeatedly told me I was special. They believed I could do anything. They were sure I would be president of the United States someday. Over time, a very strange thing happened: I believed them.

I didn't uncover the fallacy of that foundational belief until I was in my 50's. Were they lying to me? It doesn't matter. What matters is that it changed everything about my life. What I believed became the foundation that attracted other supporting beliefs. I never attempted to validate them. I liked them and they comforted me. Unconsciously, I adopted them and soon they were actionable. I learned that the root of all behavior is our belief.

Have you ever felt bullet proof? Have you felt so intuitive that you reacted instinctively to any challenge or assault? I have, and I'm calling it 'compulsive belief.' We don't know why we feel this way, but we do. It empowers us or it limits us.

Our compulsive beliefs emerge in response to situations, circumstances and moods. Simply maintaining the proper mix of business, adrenaline and caffeine could perpetuate my compulsive beliefs. It felt like success.

Those were the pendulum swings of my life. I defined my value by the number of emails I received and the demand on my schedule. I thought those two years I spent 'retired' would bring contentment and satisfaction. It was the opposite for me.

I never found enjoyment outside of work. Mowing the yard never resulted in that endorphin release. I'm not proud of the ways I tried to fill that void. I needed a mission, a distraction. I needed to feed the obsessive belief that consumed my life.

Then everything changed. After Terry and Lynnae (Melin) were married, they became the live-in managers of a 108 unit apartment complex we owned. Soon they were talking *grandchildren*. Was I old enough to be a grandparent? It didn't matter. The future Grandma Vicki informed me she had no intention of being a long-distance grandmother. The next piece of property purchased would be a haven for all future grandchildren. Ultimately, we found that property and moved 135 miles.

'We' were pregnant all over again.

The Return of My Compulsive Behavior

With the move to Bourbonnais, I wish I had focused on improving my golf game. Instead, I became a compulsive consumer of real estate and businesses. I had a significant amount of excess cash and an appetite that seemed to be satisfied by building the empire.

In any real estate project, I knew we could leverage the profitability simply by occupying more seats at the table. Often, there were good smaller players in the marketplace who we could use for flooring, signage, concrete, and so on. Those owners were often limited by their own credit facilities and the burden of administrative responsibilities. We began to acquire them and centralize their operations. We built our own I.T. department and eventually bought an I.T. and payroll company. Our human resources department served all of our own companies as well as others. Our real estate management company managed and maintained all of our properties. Even a pest control business fit nicely into the mix. We formed an electrical company, a construction company, and eventually got back into the lighting business. Along the way, we picked up this little sub shop. I'll tell you more about that later. Life was good.

I dreamed a lot of dreams. I was born to achieve. I was certain that continued growth in the real estate markets was the path to a billion dollar net worth. There was, however, one possibility my compulsive beliefs would not allow me to imagine: in all of the work, all of the business, all of the potential risk and reward, I never imagined that I could fail.

I'm not sure when it happened. I'm not sure when I began to ignore the road signs. My compulsive belief system simply stopped feeling pain or fear about the possibility of loss. I had dismissed it from my calculation; it couldn't happen to me.

I began to believe I had the answers. I believed that God had purposed me for this. Whatever happened, things would be alright.

I strayed from the business practices that brought me to the party. I became bored with the fundamentals. I only found excitement in the deals. I had highly paid people who gradually were able to tell me only what I wanted to hear.

Then came the crash of 2008. Every principle or resource needed for success was available to me, but many required change in my actions. That would require change in my beliefs as well. As the economy shifted, I simply didn't want to shift with it. I was certain that we could push our way through. I didn't want to lay off employees or scale anything back.

Most of all, I didn't want to seek advice. There were so many things I could have done, but my pride and conflicting beliefs stood in the way. Admitting I didn't have the answers was a display of weakness. Weakness leads to failure, and I was not going to fail.

Our banking relationships were friendly and open. We kept our long-term plans in play and counted the months until the economy would rebound. Everything was set. We were positioned to capitalize. We even set up a captive insurance company so we could self-insure our properties. That alone would save us nearly half a million dollars a year.

You know the old saying: "Buy when everyone else is selling. Sell when everyone else is buying." We had it all planned out. I was confident. I was firm in my belief.

I was wrong.

Chapter Six: The Raid

'My son, do not despise the Lord's discipline, and do not resent his rebuke, because the Lord disciplines those he loves, as a father the son he delights in.' (Proverbs 3: 11-12 NIV)

It was a stressful morning. Terry and I stood in my office discussing the downsizing of our construction business. I was trying to minimize the impact on people and on my pride. Terry had potent advice, driven by logic and clear financial projections. In recent months, however, I found myself stuck. I struggled to reconcile the inconsistency of my assumptions.

We always attacked, we didn't retreat. We always bought, we didn't sell. We were always blessed. I didn't want to take any action that violated what had worked in the past.

As we argued, my eyes caught movement in my spacious office. The front of our 22,500 square foot complex was covered in tinted glass. The executive offices overlooked the parking lot. It was a beautiful facility where over 45 people handled the day-to-day operations of our 14 businesses. My office had its own conference room and restroom. There were days I never left that office.

Suddenly, the parking lot was loaded with police cars. One after the other, they surrounded the building. "We better see what's going on," I said as Terry and I stared. A year before, one of our employees was arrested on a job site. I assumed this was a similar situation. What a hassle for us.

As I opened my office door, we heard men yelling for everyone to back away from their computers and move into the hallways. I saw more than a dozen officers racing around with their weapons drawn.

"Can I help you with something?" I offered to one of the men who wasn't in uniform. He seemed to be in charge.

"Mr. Yates, you need to step back into your office and don't touch anything." He forcefully ushered me toward the door. I watched as another officer ushered Terry to our main conference room.

"What's going on?" I asked.

"We are executing a search warrant," he said as he shoved a piece of paper into my hands.

I had never seen a search warrant before. I struggled to maintain control as my mind raced. "What are you looking for? We will provide you with whatever you need."

I watched men enter offices with boxes and start sweeping everything off of desks. "Should I call my attorney?" I asked as the agent handed me his card.

"That's up to you," he offered, "but we just want to ask you a couple of questions."

I had no idea what they could be looking for. I certainly didn't see myself as someone who was uncooperative with the authorities. I began attempting to answer their random questions, but I had no context. I couldn't think clearly. I was in over my head. It was a one-sided conversation. Their predetermined questions were well-rehearsed. The good cop/bad cop routine was bordering abuse. It was time to call my attorney.

My life changed instantaneously and there was nothing I could do about it. I will never forget the moment the bubble burst.

Suddenly it was impossible to stand on the foundation I had built. Now I would do battle to defend the premises of my very existence.

No matter what the end result, there would be a lot of blood spilled. I soon discovered there is no recovery from social/media accusation. To be the target of a government investigation was enough. I hadn't realized it yet, but it was all over the moment it started.

The barrage of officers were there until 3am, copying our computer network. They hauled out truckloads of documentation. How could we remain in business? How could we take care of our customers? Virtually all of the documentation we needed was now unavailable. It was an effective means to render us helpless. I learned very quickly that if the feds attack, the rest of the world follows suit.

The banks suddenly determined our risk profile was too high. Our loan documents allowed them to take every dollar we had to apply to loans. Checks were bouncing, even payroll. Every loan we had was called, and the financial ability to defend ourselves disappeared in a flash.

The concept of being innocent until proven guilty was just that: a concept. I was guilty until I could prove somehow that I was innocent. That proof would require a lot of time and money. Suddenly, I had neither.

The media took delight in the situation. They had been my allies and friends in previous years. I provided front page stories with projects and charitable activities. When I was named Business Man of the Year, I was a hero. The raid was a rare opportunity for excitement in a starved media environment. This was headline news over and over again.

No doubt, I had been aggressive in the expansion of business. Speculation and gossip were rampant. Bank fraud became a synonym for the intimation that everything I had ever done was a lie. Real estate was failing everywhere in that economic climate. Suddenly it all became my fault. Pending projects were denied payment. The actual failure came largely after the fact. Once I had been bled out, I was unable to pay bills. My accusers had created a self-fulfilling prophecy.

I Was The Frog

I remember as a boy, my dad told a joke we thought was hilarious. Now it came back in such vivid detail that I realized its true meaning. The joke goes like this.

A scientist decided to see how far a frog could jump. When he yelled, the frog jumped five feet. After recording the results, the scientist proceeded to cut off one of the frog's legs. This time, the frog jumped only 3 feet. After documenting the results, the scientist removed another leg.

Having only two legs left, the frog managed to jump 2 feet. Once again, the scientist documented his results and removed another leg. Still, the frog managed to jump almost a foot. Finally, the last leg was removed.

Despite all urging, the frog did not jump. Shaking his head, the scientist made his final notation: *Frog with no legs becomes hard of hearing.*

I was now the frog. I was expected to perform while being dissected and analysed. Despite my relentless efforts to fulfill the expectations of others, I could not. Even worse was the inability to fulfill the compulsion of my own beliefs, so heavily coupled with my need to perform and be validated by others.

Suddenly, everything I believed was contradicted and in chaos. The internal conflict was only paralleled by the chain reactions of my daily crisis.

How did it come to this?

Whatever happened from this point on, I would never be the same. My family would never be the same. My self-image would definitely never be the same.

Absorbing problems into our lives a little bit at a time seems normal. Like radiation, it only becomes a problem when we get too much, too fast. Our experiences aren't always positive or fun, but we survive them. As a general rule, we try to avoid unpleasant ones whenever we can. I had fallen off the boat of my foundational beliefs into shark-infested waters. Nobody was coming to save me.

Abruptly, people who clamored for my attention now couldn't be bothered. Every conversation revolved around the 'situation.' Every piece of information had to be carefully disseminated. The sharks weren't always easy to identify.

When the economy turned, I didn't have the answers. I was too arrogant to admit I was in trouble. Real estate deals often entered with just a signature suddenly couldn't cash flow. Banks were running from developments as fast as they could. Loans that were already approved (with construction in process) were suddenly upside-down. Banks were pulling all lines of credit. It was even more exaggerated for me because there were so many. Leveraging up was the trend. I had taken millions of dollars in cash and equity and leveraged it to the maximum. I was all in.

I watched that equity disappear in an instant. Cash flow and lines of credit vanished. I owed interest on projects that weren't cash flowing yet. I was desperate to be strong enough to get through it. Everyone thought it would last 12-18 months. Together with our banking allies, we were desperately trying to find ways to refinance. We pulled in available collateral to cover loans that otherwise would rapidly become non-performing. If we defaulted it would be a disaster for the bank and for us.

We did have one business with significant value remaining. It wasn't fully performing, but on paper it had equity. After exchanges and discussions and appraisals, it was decided to borrow heavily against that business, property, and equipment. The loan was structured to make improvements. We had the construction capability within the business we owned to perform the work ourselves, for the most part. We would take a strong profit from the work to satisfy a number of difficult financial situations. At the time, it seemed like our only solution.

It was my decision. It seemed logical. I never imagined the weight it ultimately was afforded. Unwilling to fail or look weak, I put in motion a process that was deemed to be bank fraud. By doing the work ourselves, about a third of the loan proceeds were moved outside the business as profit. My effort to prevail backfired. It was the final straw that led to my brokenness.

The End vs. The Means

Did I realize it was criminal to do this? It never occurred to me that it might be. I had convinced myself it was a logical choice. When everything hit the fan, I was never allowed to give that explanation. I entered a realm where I had no power and no voice. It was a one-way street. When you deal with the government, you are told exactly how things are going to go. I learned quickly that 'intent' was not required to be guilty.

I rationalized my actions because I believed in the end it would all 'work out.' Ultimately, the bank involved was shut down by the FDIC because they had so many real estate projects going bad. They, like many of us, had relied on a growing and profitable real estate market. Our beliefs betrayed us.

Once the bank failed, my lender was the FDIC and my case came under federal scrutiny. My legacy immediately changed from success to indictment. That process could support an entire book of its own. It's like sharks smelling blood in the water. If you can't support a massive legal team (which I couldn't afford), you are headed for a plea deal just to survive.

One by one, banks refused to do business with us. Good, long-term employees found other jobs. Customers worried whether we would be able to perform. The cascade was incredible. Still, I imagined we could recover. I imagined I could redeem myself (interesting words). With only a few small modifications, my psyche was intact and my neural pathways found a new route.

Covering over the pain receptors, mortaring in the joints, hardening the shelter, re-writing my experiences… those were the instincts of warfare and adrenaline which bobbed to the surface once, twice, finally three times…

Have you ever tried to minimize your involvement in your own failures? What if by doing so, you missed the greatest opportunity of your life?

How could I choose between rebuilding the walls of denial and allowing them to be completely destroyed?

Did I have a choice?

Perhaps you could say it was the heart attack that saved my life. You know, the heart attack that a person is 'lucky' enough to have because it doesn't kill them; the crisis that forces them to change priorities or die. The heart attack that gives them another chance to live life differently.

This was my (proverbial) 'heart attack.'

Chapter Seven: The Investigation Misdirection

Walking from the parking garage to the federal building was an out-of-body experience. Being numb seemed like the only way to make it through each day. I'd previously wondered why some people live dependent on alcohol or drugs. Now it seemed imaginable.

My attorney contacted me with the news we were to meet with the investigators. I was still in the dark about the process. They raided us and then it was silent for months. The newspapers and other detractors worked us over with beating after speculative beating. They had softened me up for the interview.

I staggered ahead in the only suit that fit me. As I walked, I remembered my discussion over the phone with the attorney: "Remember Greg, they can lie to you but you can't lie to them. They will try to get you frustrated, so just relax. We don't even know if you're the target of their investigation. Just let me guide you through the interview. If you are in question about anything, I will step in."

We were introduced to three investigators and the prosecutor, who then left for other meetings. The investigators began asking me questions about transactions, loans and projects specifically related to the bank in question. Then they gave me the head fake.

"We understand what has happened to you, Mr. Yates. You aren't alone. This is what we call a 'hub conspiracy.' The bank was at the center of this and you were just one of the many spokes of the wheel. They did this same thing with several other people, and we need to know everything you know about how this happened."

I assured them I would do my best to walk through the process as honestly as I could recall. I was so relieved because they realized I had not intentionally defrauded anyone. That was what mattered, right? I wanted to be vindicated, and it felt good for them to say they understood. I failed to realize that their understanding and how they would treat me were two completely separate issues.

I was low-hanging fruit. There was an easy conviction to be had. I was giving them every piece of information to make it an open and shut case. All they had to do was put me at ease, convince me that I was the victim, convince me that I was helping them understand where things went wrong.

I assured them that everyone in the process had been trying to do the right thing. The bank was trying to keep their loans on real estate from going bad. As business men, we were trying to sustain until the economy recovered. I shook their hands and walked out with my attorney. We recapped outside. He concurred that they were not after me. Once again, we had no idea how wrong we would be.

The News

Months passed. We sold our primary corporate office building as we dwindled down to only a few key people and businesses. Very quickly, the atrophy of this process had created its own self-fulfilling prophecy. I assured everyone that the government was not after me, but the controlled crash continued.

It was late one evening in August, more than a year after we had been raided. I was the last one in the building and had been working a job on the CNC (computer numerically controlled) machining center. It was good therapy after a long day battling senselessly in the office.

My cell phone rang with a contact of mine at the newspaper. Joel had always been a friend, so I didn't hesitate to answer.

"Greg?"

"Yes, this is Greg."

"Hi, it's Joel. I called to get a comment from you about your indictment today. It just came across the wire."

My heart stopped, my ears throbbed, and for a moment I thought I might collapse.

"Greg, can you give us a comment?"

I struggled to speak. It would be the last call I would accept from the media. My friends had become my adversaries. The calm I had felt for months had been an illusion.

I hung up and called my attorney. He hadn't heard a word about it either. Myself and my son, Terry, had become the simplest exit from this case for the government. The indictment was real and the firestorm would begin again.

What do you do when you don't even recognize the man in the mirror? Everything I knew about myself was wrong. Everything I thought I had influence over was wrong. Everything I knew about how to get things done… was wrong.

Suddenly I had to revisit every conversation with every remaining lender, every customer, and every employee. I had been so certain that we were not the target of their investigation. Now it seemed to everyone that I had been lying. I had worked to put their minds at ease.

People who owed us money rationalized withholding it. Anyone who needed an excuse for their own struggles could point to me. Our home and any remaining revenue streams became the next targets. I couldn't afford to pay my attorneys and now I needed more of them.

Looking back on all of this, I wonder if I should have just given up and thrown up my hands. At the time, there was no way I could do it. I imagined that I would somehow emerge on the other side with some form of justification.

I was flailing in the wind; shadow boxing and being blindsided until I could no longer feel the punches or the pain. I was dead and yet I kept walking.

A Few Good Men

Every conversation in public became an endless loop of my 'situation.' I couldn't go anywhere or talk to anyone without the black hole of indictment draining all my energy and focus.

I know I'm not the only one to go through this anomaly, but I had never imagined it. I struggled to go to church because I had gone from an arrogant posture to a void so deep I couldn't express it. I felt mocked and angry when I tried to worship.

I couldn't ask anyone to support me. I didn't deserve it. The church didn't know what to do with me. By and large, the church was not open to me.

I don't blame anyone. I didn't deserve love or forgiveness. I remember how unapproachable I had become. I can't imagine very many people felt like poking the bear.

Embracing the few who reached out was difficult. Feeling unworthy was hard. I had wondered for so many years who my real friends were. My cynical beliefs assumed that everyone was looking for something. Yet here they were, when everything had fallen apart.

Business people, many of whom I'd never met personally, wanted to meet. Some came by for coffee just to affirm me. "Greg, hold your head up. You may have failed, but you are not a failure." I cried uncontrollably. Some were awkward and didn't know what to say, but they still came. They blew me away.

I remember one businessman coming by my office, talking about a similar legal situation he had some twenty years previously. Even in my haze, I knew God was reaching out to me through these men. It wasn't easy for them, and I respected them for it. I hoped that I could be that kind of man.

I didn't know how I could keep getting up in the morning to walk through this putrid stench again and again. I didn't see any options. Maybe this really was the valley of the shadow of death.

For the first time, the compulsive beliefs of my life were silent. Without their strength, I really did feel fear.

I had been operating under misdirection during the last few months. Struggling in this bed of fear, however, I realized the misdirection had been part of my life much longer than I cared to admit. Abruptly, the questions had no answers.

- Is it possible God has abandoned me?

- Has my value become obsolete?

- Have my assumptions about my relationship with God and His purpose for me been flawed?

One thing I knew for certain: despite extreme success, I had never felt the peace He promised. Perhaps it was time to question everything. Through my brokenness, the beliefs of my heart had become pliable. I wondered if it was possible that my previous beliefs were flawed.   I could no longer defend the misdirection of my life.

Chapter Eight: Flying Blind

I was PIC (pilot in command) in my Saratoga during this time of searching. I was alone and it was complete IMC (instrument meteorological conditions). You couldn't even see outside the cockpit, and yet I was flying along at a good 160kph (knots per hour).

The drone of the engine always comforted me. I had long since lost any fear of instrument flying. I suppose as a general rule I had no sense of fear about anything, except that one lingering question which somehow shook me. I had another hour of darkness to pierce. Even though I was flying in familiar territory, the quiet voice of despair began to crowd my thoughts.

…Greg… this is just like your life. You're flying along as fast as you can and you don't realize you are in the clouds. You don't know what is ahead. You don't know if there is another aircraft out there that isn't flying in the system. You don't know if there is wind shear ahead of you that will throw you into a dangerous attitude, or hail that could cause irrecoverable damage. Yet, you have faith in this airplane, in your abilities, in your past experience, and you keep flying on.

How can you have so much faith in yourself and so little faith in me? Perhaps today is the day you will meet me, face-to-face.

It was as clear as anything I have ever experienced. I was moved, yet I was fiercely defiant. I believed in God and His purpose for my life. It simply wasn't possible for me to make such a transition to total surrender, especially not with all the commitments

I had made. With all of the plans and plates spinning in motion, I still gripped my obsessive beliefs like a security blanket.

Without those personal performance mechanisms I would have nothing. I would *be* nothing. I felt the gripping panic set in. The house of emotional cards was carefully built. I was afraid to move even one of them.

'Do not fear for I have redeemed you. I have summoned you by name and you are mine. When you pass through the waters, I will be with you' when you pass through the rivers, they will not sweep you away. When you walk through the fire, you will not be burned. The flames will not set you ablaze for I am the lord your God.' (Isaiah 43:1-3a NIV)

And there it was again: that haunting, unanswerable question I avoided so effectively. The power of it was debilitating. Answering it was impossible. Why even ask it? And yet, I hungered for it, feared it, and couldn't stop asking myself:

"Am I the man I was created to be?"

In the desperateness of it all, the noise of it all, the euphoria of it all at times, I knew my life was meant to be more than this emptiness. Wasn't my faith enough? Wasn't I more capable, more powerful, and more successful than almost everyone I knew? Hadn't God blessed me more than others?

Yet here I was, wrapped in uncertainty. The nucleus of my life was grasping for a self-igniting restart to it all. The question was real; it became the consuming thought and prayer of my life. "Lord, make me the man you created me to be."

Desperate Weakness (March 13, 2013 — a year before I knew I would be going to prison)

I didn't realize the indictment was your answer to my prayer when I began praying that I could become the man you BUILT ME TO BE. I prayed it out of desperation in my hopeless moments, when I felt I could not resist the power of sin. Sometimes I prayed it simply because of the tiresome feelings that covered me, realizing that one day just fades into another and it all goes round and round, over and over with nothing that really matters.

I knew you, God. I used to feel so close to you. So real in your presence and full of desire to make a difference in the lives of others. You blessed me richly in so many ways. Money, strength, power. Everything I ever wanted. I always felt strong and powerful, and I acknowledged that my gifts and strength came from you, didn't I? Wasn't that the idea?

Why did you pull away from me? I really did believe you were using me, and that you could use me. But I was empty. I had done things I wasn't proud of. I allowed myself to be seduced by my own success, I guess. To be honest, Lord, I hated myself and I knew I had hurt the family and others, no matter how I tried not to.

I was supposed to be Superman. I was supposed to be strong enough for everyone to lean on. That was my only identity and I thought it was from you.

Still, Lord, I pray that you can use me. Lord, make me the man you built me to be. Transform me into the person you intended me to be; the person you created me to be. I feel strangely excited about the possibility. I wasn't willing to do this by myself, I remember that. Now I don't want to go back. I don't ever want to go back.

My Hot Tub Experience

I was broken and vulnerable, but I was in pursuit of something I had never successfully achieved. I was pursuing peace.

I found it in my hot tub on December 28, 2012, 16 months before I knew I was going to prison. I finally self-surrendered (prison terminology). It wasn't much of a choice, really. God said He did everything for our salvation. In my case, He really did.

He moved every obstacle, ripped off every band aid, removed every distraction. I felt as if I was with Jesus in the garden. Everything about my life had come to this moment. I had to receive what God had for me, or I had to abandon Him completely.

At this point, I had no power, no ability to fight on, no desire or passion left. I was completely broken.

I asked the family to understand that I was taking 10 days to seek my own personal Pentecost. I spent that time pouring myself out to God. Yelling, praying, agonizing, and talking to God on my knees all day and night. Finally, one early morning in the cold air, I retreated to the hot tub outside our bedroom. I could talk to the Lord there without waking Vicki. I couldn't sleep. I was desperate beyond desperate. I wasn't asking for anything any longer, I simply had to know if He was really there. I had to know if He had more for me. I had to know if he really could give me peace and if there really was purpose beyond my brokenness.

I cried out to God while the steam rose up around me. I finally reached the point of complete desperation. "God, if you have more for me as a man, I want it. If you created me to be more than I have become, please direct me. If I have completely failed you and missed your plan for my life, I understand. I still love you and I know I don't deserve anything more than this. I will do my best to serve you."

And that was it. I was completely empty. It was as if I had finally released every thread of belief and watched it drift away as steam up into the sky. I struggled to climb out of the hot tub and quietly dragged myself in to bed. The year was almost over, and perhaps my life was as well. I had made mistakes, I had sinned. I had missed and squandered opportunities that could not be recovered. I lived in the idolatry of my own compulsive beliefs. I had placed myself on the throne of my kingdom. I struggled to care whether I lived or died. In fact, in many ways, I was already dead.

I woke to a new day, late but peaceful. I felt a peace that had no explanation; an optimism that had no underlying 'deal' or 'wealth effect' associated with it. I cautiously felt as if God had done something.

The basis for my past beliefs had been largely developed on circumstantial evidence. Now, it had shifted instantaneously in a supernatural way. I knew God had done whatever was necessary. He accomplished what I could not do. I was afraid to test it. I just kept holding on to it. A curious giddy giggle found its way into the New Year.

Have you ever struggled with the lament of failure which tormented you endlessly? Haven't you wished that you could've resolved your issues on your own? I desperately wanted to save the day, yet I couldn't. I was fixated on my own ability to define my beliefs until God's grace made His power perfect in me.

I wasn't flying blind in the clouds any longer. Now I was building on the true cornerstone. I had found the foundation of all transformational belief.

'But he said to me, "My grace is sufficient for you, for my power is made perfect in weakness." Therefore I will boast all the more gladly about my weaknesses, so that Christ's power may rest on me.' (2 Corinthians 12: 9 NIV)

Chapter Nine: The Valley of the Shadow of Death

A year had passed since my indictment. Once again, I was traveling north to my attorney's office to meet with my accusers. Sometime in the week prior to another court status date, a token meeting would take place to feign the process of moving my case along. The investigators had long since moved on to new targets.

My attorney calmly shared his experience in over thirty years of dealing with the government. "Once they have indicted you, Greg, they really have no intention of taking your case to trial. It's too much work. If they have to go to trial, the prosecutor will be very upset. The day will come when you will either make a deal with them to plead guilty, or we will have to start insisting on a trial. The odds are stacked against you. The only way you can ever be 'not guilty' is to go to trial. But, if you go to trial and lose, the results will be much worse."

The weariness of these trips drained me. I struggled to maintain my commitments. I pulled into the parking lot, thankful to be alone. With a deep sigh, I lifted a feeble prayer: "Lord, help me to embrace whatever you have for me today. Speak through me because I can't speak for myself. Grant me wisdom because I don't trust my own wisdom any longer. Help me to honor you and trust your plan. Amen."

As I took the elevator to the second floor, I thought about the process. Being in court the next day, debating logic with passionate arguments, was fantasy. In reality, the process was designed to take years and typically win by default. Why did they need to throw punches at me when survival was barely manageable? I couldn't even afford to pay my attorney. Eventually, time would exhaust my resources, and they knew that all too well.

After about twenty minutes of redundant conversation, the investigator was done. "I don't really have any more questions, so we will see you in court in a few days."

It wasn't planned, but suddenly I blurted it out: "How much longer is it going to take to get this behind us?" Everyone froze.

The investigator sat back down. "Well," he started, "I think it is probably going to take another two to three years."

I couldn't help myself. I jumped up and shot back at him uncharacteristically, "I can't wait another two or three years. I can't keep living like this. I can't keep paying my attorneys for another two or three years."

My attorney put his hand on my arm. "We will work on that, Greg. You don't have to worry about how you will pay us." As if that was really the biggest issue.

I had forgotten one of the first things my attorney told me when this process started. Now, it surfaced. "Greg, there are three things you need to know about this process. First, they can lie to you but you can't lie to them. Second, they will stick you and then wait for you to bleed out. Third, there will come a day when you will have to decide if you want to go to trial or make a deal."

I was defiant when it all started, but now I was willing to play along. I watched the investigator eyeball me. "Well, Mr. Yates, we can put together a plea deal if you want to change your plea to guilty. That's the other option."

"I'd like to see it," I said. With that, the notes were closed. I had taken the bait. That was the inevitable day they were waiting for. I broke ranks and showed that I was beaten. I walked out realizing that my fate was in their hands. Their 98% conviction rate was intact. I handed them my head for their trophy wall.

Making the Deal

A "plea deal" sounded simple enough. First, you have to change your plea to guilty. That's when the sickening feeling begins. The agreement reiterates that you *knew* what you were doing was wrong, and you did it anyway. You intentionally defrauded the bank. Then it proceeds to make it clear that you are forfeiting all of your rights, including appeals. There is no chance to change your mind. Finally, you read to the end and discover no matter what deal you make with the prosecutors, the judge has the final say. He can still do whatever he wants.

I hadn't intentionally defrauded anyone. Now, in order to get this done, I had to intentionally lie. I had to be criminal in order to plead guilty to a crime I didn't know I was committing. It was gut-wrenching, and yet I really had no choice. I rationalized I had known what I was doing, even if I didn't realize it was criminal.

I sat in front of the magistrate, an administrative judge who handles this sort of thing. "Mr. Yates, has anyone coerced you into changing your plea?"

Gulp. Another lie would be required. "No, Your Honor."

And the newspaper presses queued up again with more fuel to print. Yates Pleads Guilty. Former Business Man of the Year Faces up to 30 Years in Prison.

I remember the gist of a poem an older man in our church used to quote. "Life is like sticking your hand in a bucket of water. You can stir it around and splash all you want, but when you pull your hand out, the hole that's left is how much you'll be missed when you're gone." We laughed and joked about that old guy. We were young and we had no perspective. Counting down the days until the sentencing reminded me of its harsh truth.

It's impossible to console your wife and family when you can't even get your mind around it yourself. In effect, I lied about everything I was feeling the entire time. There was no point handling it any differently. It's like being sick and everyone asking how you are feeling: you're sick.; you feel sick.

I knew there was life beyond this process, but I was in a holding pattern. I was determined not to crash physically, mentally or emotionally. I was desperately grasping for the peace God had given me.

They tell me faith is the essence of things not seen. It seemed most often like a mirage. It popped up once in a while and then vanished. I saw myself walking on the water. I tried, in faith, to walk toward Jesus. Most often I succumbed to the raging storm.

How do you convince yourself and others of something you can't see? And if you can't see it, how can you believe? Is it a fairytale or is it the great cloud of witnesses cheering you on? It was an agonizing, sleepless reoccurrence.

How do you hold on to hope when everything you thought was important is gone? How do you face yourself in the mirror when all you can see is your failure and mistakes? I had every chance in the world to get it right. God had blessed me more than anyone I'd ever met. Still, I managed to blow it. I hated who I had become and how I had arrived there. I hated my arrogance and my pursuit of egotistical gain. There wasn't enough left inside me to power my shields. I was empty. I was waiting for the Grim Reaper to show up. I was ready to face the last penalty for my pathetic life of failure, pride and sin.

He never came.

Living With Nothing to Lose

I remember being asked an interesting question while attending a seminar. "If you knew you could not fail, what would you do?" What an interesting question. I always relied on my past compulsive beliefs for a response. The next achievement was always based on my view of the past. Now, I wasn't sure how to answer.

While I waited for sentencing, it occurred to me that perhaps I should ask that question one more time. What would I do if I knew I could not fail?

Let's face it: I really had nothing left to lose. Trying to protect my accumulation of past successes had likely led me here in the first place. I was willing to do whatever it took to protect my assets, rather than allow myself to look the truth squarely in the eye. In the midst of dealing with the liquidation of my *life*, it was as if I was planning my own funeral. I would even attend the ceremony and hear the gavel drop. But, I wouldn't really be dead. I might actually be more prepared to live than I had ever been.

I set myself free from the expectation of being restored. Simultaneously, I was a failure and a success. I was broken to the point of violent physical agony, and yet I was beginning to see that there was a limit to the clutches of fear; a limit that required me to hang on and to believe.

Approaching the sentencing date, May 16, 2014, I still clung to the possibility that I might not get any actual jail time. It was a luxury my attorney and the prosecutor allowed me to indulge in. Perhaps it keeps you more cooperative and more congenial.

No matter what happened in the process, I was not going to let it take my newfound peace from me. I was not going to hate the people involved. I was not going to be angry at anyone except myself. Even though I was just a piece of meat in the grinder, I could hold on to my faith. I was determined to treat everyone with respect.

We entered the federal building early, suits on and a heightened sense of mixed emotion. I told my parents not to come, but that wasn't going to happen. My supporters were the only observers in the gallery. There were no 'victims' in my particular case, since it was a single loan inherited by the FDIC.

I waited for the hearing to begin. It was as if time had slowed to a crawl. I looked over the courtroom and thought of the many things that had occurred in this room. I stared at the magnificent seal of the United States of America behind the judge's chair. It chilled me to realize that today I was considered an adversary of the very country I loved and would die for. It was hard to swallow.

Everyone assembled today because of my actions. No matter how badly I wanted to change the past, there was no way to do it. I could only submit myself to the authority at hand. There were no more decisions to make on my part. There were no more future dates or possibilities of reprieve. In a matter of minutes, I would return to my family or I would be incarcerated. I was conscious of every breath and every heartbeat. Only God could negotiate on my behalf.

As we waited for the judge to enter, I was accosted with one overwhelming thought: no matter what man sat on that judgment seat, only God was truly in charge. He knew this outcome already and had made provision for it. As impossible as it seemed, I really didn't need to fear. I felt a calm that suddenly brought me out of the numbness I had been surviving in. My thoughts were clear. My confidence engaged as it had not done in a very long time.

I didn't know what the sentencing would be, but I knew one thing for certain: God was in control. He now was going to reveal His plan for my life. Whatever it was, I was ready. I felt His presence. It was time to let go; time for me to embrace my destiny which laid somewhere beyond these hellish flames.

Don't Worry About What You'll Say

There were several preparatory steps in the weeks prior to sentencing. We had the chance to gather character letters in support of me as a person. Was I a career criminal? Had I contributed to society in a positive way? I had dozens of letters from amazing supporters.

Secondly, I gave my attorney information related to all of my accomplishments, education, lifestyle, charities, boards, etc. He would give a presentation about me to help the judge understand more than just the result of my worst days. I was also told that I could make a statement during sentencing if I wanted to.

My attorney typically discouraged people from addressing the judge. In my case, he left the decision up to me. I was overloaded with emotion, but I knew I had to speak. I wrote and prepared what I might say, then gave it to my attorney for approval. He told me that if I could not finish, he would read my statement.

After reading all of the charges and my guilty plea, the judge gave my attorney a chance to speak. I watched as the judge rolled his eyes at my accomplishments. He nonchalantly acknowledged that he had read the supporting letters of recommendation. As my attorney began to plead my case, the judge practically came out of his chair. He yelled at my attorney and silenced him. "Mr. Yates has pled guilty and I will not hear any arguments to the contrary. We are not here to try this case, we are here to determine the sentence for his guilt."

I knew we were in trouble. My attorney could barely get a word out. The judge was angry and indignant. I had heard of his reputation and I knew this was not a good sign. They began reading

70

the computation for my sentence. They believed I should receive 51-61 months in prison. I knew there would be a reduction because I had made the plea deal, but its leverage seemed long forgotten.

The overwhelming nature of this past hour was coming to a head. I was going to have the chance to speak. All I could do was pray that God would empower me. I prayed that I could speak the words that would lift up Christ, and if possible, impact this hearing for our good.

"Mr. Yates," the judge brought me to attention. "You certainly don't have to do this, but if you would like to make a statement, you can do so at this time."

"Yes Sir, I would," I replied, and stood. I walked to the podium. I had spoken and sung in front of thousands of people many times. Perhaps they were all in preparation for this very moment. This was unlike any forum I had ever attended, much less spoken to. All eyes were on me.

"Please proceed when you are ready," the judge said. "Take your time."

It was a carefully worded speech that, if I'd read from my writing, would have lasted three or four minutes. I was shocked to find out I'd actually spoken for closer to 25 minutes. I couldn't have planned that, but in the moment there was incredible power. I knew it was divine.

I remember telling the judge that I took full responsibility for everything that had happened. It overwhelmed me that these proceedings, including his own involvement, was my fault. I broke down as I talked about my parents being in the courtroom. They raised me right and believed in me, and now I was forcing them to endure so much pain. I talked about my family and all of the people who had lost their jobs because of my actions. Because of my actions, all my past achievements were negated. As far as I was concerned, I was starting over.

"But, Your Honor, I'm not dead. This simply cannot define my life. This cannot keep me from becoming what God has created me to become. That is the one thing I know with all of my heart. I promise you that I will pursue it with all of my being for the rest of my life. I have so much to make up for. I owe a debt to so many. I owe a debt to God himself."

Terry was to be sentenced after me. I talked about his role and his age (only 29) when all of these things happened. He was operating under my authority, doing what I told him to do. He believed in me. He did not deserve to be punished. I begged the judge to take whatever punishment he believed was appropriate and apply it to me.

I still cry as I emotionally re-live those moments. I was broken before the judge and it wasn't something I could control. I gave myself over to my judgment and asked for mercy. In conclusion, I thanked the judge for his indulgence and his consideration. I knew I would be able to repay the loan in question if I could work rather than go to prison.

As I progressed through my statement, things changed. The judge visibly migrated from his paperwork. We locked eyes in my penitent exchange. I did not argue, I did not blame. I went out of my way to show specific respect for the prosecutor and all involved in the process. I was sincere. It was my decision-making and my brokenness that led to this event. I had nobody else to blame. Still, I surprisingly felt I had a foundation beneath me.

The judge gave me latitude when I broke down and had to regain my composure. He locked in with me as I talked about my family. I saw him smile a couple of times as we traveled together.

I don't remember everything I said. I've tried to get a transcript of the statement because I would love to read what happened. In my Spirit-led openness, I spoke. And eventually I was done.

I thanked the judge and walked to my seat. I felt released. It was as if I had just stepped out of the hot tub experience once again. I knew that God was in control. Whatever happened was for my good.

As I sat, the judge began to speak. He hesitated at first, looking for the words. "In my 28 years sitting on this bench, I have never heard a more heartfelt and sincere statement. Mr. Yates, (pause), I believe you. I believe that you are genuinely sorry for what has happened. And I believe that you, indeed, will make a difference with your life."

I'm not sure whether or not I was breathing. He was looking into my eyes as if we were the only ones in the courtroom. I wondered if other defendants actually looked into the eyes of the judge. I couldn't help myself. We were men, posed in this environment for different reasons, but we were both men nonetheless. I had appealed to him as a man and as a father. I had spoken from the heart and he had heard me. After thousands of statements, and likely a numbness to the process, one statement had rung true in his spirit and he was taking the time to acknowledge it. I knew that the Spirit of all men's spirit had spoken. I wondered what He had said.

"I know I am going to be criticized for this," the judge continued, "but I like to believe that I give, what I believe, is appropriate sentencing to each case." He proceeded to tell the story of several previous cases which were similar to mine. In each of those cases, the defendants had received 3-5 years in prison. The entire room held its breath as he spoke. The scope of my future was being defined. It did not look favorable.

"However," he continued, "I believe in this case, while it is impossible for me to justify only supervised release, the appropriate sentence is one year and one day in the Federal Prison Camp in Oxford, Wisconsin."

It seems hard to imagine, but at that point I felt like giving him a hug. The weight could have been so much heavier. The year and a day sentence, I learned later, also allowed me to get good time. It reduced my likely time of incarceration to around ten months.

It was a moment we could never forget. We had weathered the storm. We had a clear timeframe now. In nine weeks, I would report. I hated the path, but I thanked God. I knew without a doubt that He had orchestrated it.

I was embarking on another countdown, but this time I felt purpose hiding behind the shadow. It was an unthinkable next 12 months, but it had already been almost three years since the process had begun. There was nothing left but to embrace the path and learn the lessons I had been taken aside to learn.

I was broken, but I knew there was healing in the path ahead. Healing for my body, mind and soul. Healing for my faith. I felt the twinkle of possibility that I could become the man I was created to be.

Chapter Ten: Powerless

'When I am afraid, I put my trust in you. In God, whose word I praise; in God I trust and am not afraid. <u>What can mere mortals do to me</u>?' (Psalm 56: 3-4 NIV)

We ambled quietly north in the truck as the day had arrived. Like the countdown of a death sentence the past couple of months had flown by, just as life does. I tried to make every day count, every meal, every ray of sunlight, every moment with the family. Disbelief and fear of the unknown had clinched tightly around my intestines. I worked to quip and hide any discomfort from the family, especially from Vicki.

She would be dropping me off and heading home to spend the bulk of the next year living alone. I knew there would be endless shrapnel continuing to fall. She had to deal with it and still try to pay the bills, all while her husband of 35 years was gone.

Her constant strength had seen us through what most would consider a long married life. During the past few months I had woken many times with the deep, searing realization of the pain I had caused her. In return, she offered undeniable proof of her enduring love.

She deserved so much more. I had failed her not just by being too proud to properly deal with the decisions I had made, but in so many more ways. I had isolated myself from her. I made judgements about her that were driven by my compulsive need to protect my vulnerable heart.

I built emotional walls to keep every feeling under control. My emotions were like a piece of metal. In the face of my crumbling self-image, the flood waters of uncontrollable emotion came crashing in. No longer could I deny who I had become. No longer could I justify the insensitivities and rationalizations.

The overwhelming and random outpouring of it all was like water pouring on the desert. I could not stop its instant absorption into my soul. When it came in floods, it destroyed every bridge I'd built.

I tried to re-establish the calm and calculated self I had known. Again and again the waves tore down my attempts. The nakedness of my condition forced me to stare straight into the face of truth.

I didn't even know myself. I was *not* the man I thought I was. No amount of denial and depression could restore the force fields of my previous life. They had been the only security and means of defense I had ever known.

The powerful and familiar belief system which had driven me for so long was broken beyond repair and I was going to prison. Nothing I could do would change that.

My life would be changed forever. As we got closer to the prison, the little boy in me wanted to run away. It felt like the end of my life. It would be the longest day I had ever known.

Self-Surrender

The process is called 'self-surrender.' You show up, identify yourself and surrender to whatever process lies ahead. If there is anything that could be done to further humiliate you, I'm not sure what it would be.

Do people *really* try to sneak things into prison by hiding them in body cavities? In prison, 'one size fits all.' If a murderer or violent offender has to be subject to it, you do too, Mr. Bank Fraud 18303-026. Bend and squat. Even if it is just for our amusement. We are going to teach you just 'where you are' and how irrelevant your past is now.

You are an inmate. You cannot be trusted. You will do exactly as you are told, when you are told. At 55, I was accustomed to a somewhat different lifestyle; a certain degree of basic respect and civility. I was used to an acknowledgement of who I am, not a green uniform that looks just like everyone else.

My head was spinning. I was led down the hallways, getting a tour of the facility from Ted, the office orderly. I stared into the faces of intimidating men; I had always been the one who intimidated others. I heard the F word more times in my first evening than I had heard in my entire life. We're not in Kansas anymore.

Floating mindlessly, nodding to what was being said, I was led to a 10x10 cell where three guys were waiting. The 4pm count had just cleared. They were my new cellmates. My bunk was on top, barely wide enough for my shoulders.

At that moment, I didn't have a perspective of the gift God had given me in Tim, Marty and Jeff, but I would soon learn. From helping me figure out how to climb to my bunk (at 55, weighing 268lbs), to filling out my first commissary sheet and corralling me for the necessary learning processes of prison. I found out quickly that you don't learn anything from the system. You learn it all from the inmates.

These guys were to be my family and we would take care of each other. We were all on a level playing field and nobody was impressed by anyone else's pedigree or past. We were criminals. We would carve out survival and if possible, camaraderie.

I had surrendered in every possible way. I no longer wanted to power my own life. My beliefs were in complete submission to God just as my body was in submission to incarceration. I knew there had to be purpose for this time, but I was powerless to fulfill my own destiny. The thought of infusing my own strength made me want to vomit. I was done building on a foundation of personal performance. I was ready to submit completely to whatever purpose I had been created to fulfill.

8-22-14 Journaling From Prison

I have nothing of myself worth anything, Lord. You are everything. In my emptiness and brokenness, let me find an audience in your presence. Your will be done in my surrendered life.

It's not that I am afraid, Father. I am embarrassed. I walked in the blessings of Almighty God and I viewed it selfishly and failed to see the way you could have used me. I hear you say, 'I can use you now, Greg. I am not limited. I am God and my purpose does not fail. I know you and I have brought you on this path. Together we will suffer and will exalt the name of Jesus as the way. Many will see and believe.'

Oh Lord, please grant me the days and the chance to add to the record of my life with the things you do through me, and not just my own failures. I know you remember them no more against me but help to build a new record by your Grace that is meaningful for eternity, both in praise and in leading others to the way.

11-6-14 Journaling in Prison

Good morning, Lord. You are all I have today. My focus is on you alone. You know how difficult it is for me to stop the striving. You know how much I want to work.

It is difficult to just rest in things I don't understand. It goes against everything in me, Lord. But I trust you, and I have learned how wonderful it is to live in your blessing and your peace.

It is pretty scary from a human perspective. You said you understand us better than we understand ourselves, so please remember how it is. How I am.

It feels completely irresponsible of me when I think about just letting go and trusting whatever you are doing. Trusting whatever just 'happens.' That just feels wrong with everything in me, Lord. Even here in prison, I find myself looking for ways to change things, to improve things. I stress over things that don't make sense.

Here… Now… in this place… Yes, I rest in you. I do it because I have no choice at all. That bothers me, Lord. It feels incredible and I still feel guilty. I feel like I should be doing something. On the other hand, I feel guilty because I know that this peace you have given me, this freedom, has come only because my hands are tied behind my back. I don't deserve it. I didn't earn it and I don't know how I got here except by my brokenness. How can that make sense?

Am I so untrustworthy in my own instincts that I will never be able to do anything but wait upon you? Don't get me wrong, Lord. I want your peace. In fact, this is the best I have felt about life and about us in a very long time. I want that. I want that more than anything.

I try to picture that in the business world. I really do. Help me to see it. I try to picture what it would be like having various obstacles in business and deadlines and brainstorming various options to overcome them; the excitement of it and the urgency.

How do I know what you are doing? How do I know what you want me to do? In the past, I have prayed hard over some of those things, but even when I felt you were giving me a sense that you would work it out, when the deadlines came I had to make decisions. So, I made them. Where did I go wrong?

I am here in this monastery of prison to learn from you. I am yours, Lord. Use me. Help me to trust no matter what. Help me to follow your principles and place my faith in what YOU have said, not in my own understanding.

If you take me there, I know you will have a purpose. Thank you, Lord. I needed that today.

Chapter Eleven: Finish What You Started in Me, Lord

'Create in me a pure heart, O God, and renew a steadfast spirit within me.' (Psalm 51: 10 NIV)

"So, what do you think?"

I knew she was talking, but as usual, my mind was a million miles away. Have you ever been driving and suddenly become aware that miles have passed without you realizing it? You've apparently navigated your way safely through traffic robotically.

"What?" After 25 years of marriage, Vicki couldn't be fooled. She was all too familiar with my distant look and preoccupied mind. I had agreed to take the trip, but I couldn't escape the workload that still consumed my thoughts. Honestly, I have no idea what particular crisis was going on then, but whatever it was, it seemed really important at the time. That was always the case. More vacations, family time and truly important dates had been missed because of those 'critical' issues that absolutely had to be taken care of.

It wasn't that I didn't love being with her. I really wanted to make this trip. We were headed by car through Niagara Falls to Boston, then around New England to see the rare beauty of the northeastern United States in the fall season. Still, without a distinct purpose for the day, my mind felt like there was a rheostat going off, humming like a dimmer switch until the light gets turned 'all the way up.'

"Thanksgiving dinner," she continued. "Don't you think it would be beautiful to collect some fall leaves and spread them around the table as decoration for Thanksgiving?"

FLASH. I can do this. A moment of potential purpose flashed through my brain and a familiar groove kicked in. It might not be a mind map, but I felt the possibility of a mission coming on. Purpose, action, searching. I could buy into that.

"That sounds great," I finally responded, scanning the horizon. We were traveling the back roads of New Hampshire and each rise gave birth to new amazement. Now my eyes found focus and reconnected with my brain to live in the moment. Soon, that Mercedes was in ditches and going up side trails. Somewhere there are pictures of me climbing over fences and up the limbs of trees because the color looked really unique 'up there.' We packed a lot of leaves into the car. I was excited because I was accomplishing something, especially something that was important to my girl.

I also noticed something very interesting and unexpected in the process. For some reason, those leaves looked a lot more beautiful on the tree and from a distance. What seemed like brilliant color or unique palettes of red or orange, really didn't look that way once I got close to them.

My pursuit of the color for which I had careened off the beaten path, was never exactly fulfilled. I kept trying. In fact, some of the ones that looked the most colorful were really crumbling and dead. Not at all as they appeared, calling to me on the highway.

I was obsessive in my quest to pursue my beliefs about life. Just like searching for those perfect leaves, my objective never quite looked like I envisioned. The mission itself? That was another story. The compulsion to work, to strive toward an objective... that was somehow able to release in me the sense of satisfaction I was drawn to. It was the drug of choice (combined, of course, with adrenaline and caffeine). For some reason, that striving convinced me of my own worth and validity.

Obsessions became compulsive pursuits which could be completed to satisfy my urges. From a human and business standpoint, it served me well. Was it business or was it simply busyness? I suppose if you live for the MISSION, then any ol' mission will do.

I never saw that, by the way. It was counterintuitive because my entire identity was based on accomplishment. This disconnect was never resolved until my entire belief system was broken.

'What shall we say then, that the Gentiles who did not pursue righteousness have obtained it, a righteousness that is by faith, but the children of Israel who pursued the law as the way of righteousness have not attained their goal. Why not, because they pursued it not by faith, as if it were by works.' (Romans 9:30 NIV)

Obsession *is* the Mission

I could hear the clanking of dishes in the sink as I pulled back the sheets to climb into bed. It was nearly midnight and I had to get up at 4:30. The guests had left and 'as usual' Vicki was cleaning up. She wasn't working outside the home at that time and I was running on very little sleep. Still, it bothered me to climb into bed while she was working.

"Hey baby, are you coming to bed?" I yelled.

"In a minute," she called back. I knew what that meant. They say that opposites attract, but Vicki and I were both obsessive. We were just obsessive about different things.

She never asked me to help, but it was impossible for me to go to sleep when it sounded like the 'borrowers' were working the house over. I had lived through a few of these episodes. I had so much guilt (ahhh... guilt and duty... my favorite motivators) that I finally went in to help. There was a lot of grumbling.

"Can't this wait 'til morning?" I grunted. She didn't hesitate or answer.

With the last dish I was ready to turn out the lights, and then I found out the rest of the story. Not only did the dishes have to be done, but the entire house had to be cleaned before she would go to bed. What complete nonsense.

Whenever you came to our house, night or day, it was clean enough to eat off the floor. I was always proud of that. I suppose somehow I thought we had built a self-cleaning house, or that the kids were just super neat (a fallacy that has been dispelled). It never occurred to me that the same characteristics which were keeping me from going to bed were the characteristics that kept our house (and later on our businesses) picture perfect all the time.

I could see this was not going to change, so gradually my programming began to adapt. A definite paradigm shift had to occur in my thinking. I was living with a woman who believed the architectural digest folks could show up any moment for a photo-op. I am adaptive, if nothing else. My project planning kicked in. Ah, another mission. Now I get it. This is something I can relate to.

During an evening of entertaining guests, I couldn't help noticing things that were getting out of place, and cleaning them up. When cups or glasses or plates sat unattended, I scooped them up and put them where they belonged. I became a fan of fancy 'disposable' plates and glasses for those occasions. By the time the last person left, I had allowed Vicki to say the goodbyes while I completed a sweep of the house. My mission included collecting any evidence of outside involvement. That left a quick sink of dishes (she washed, I dried and put them away) and we were off to bed.

So, what's the point, Greg? Hey, we all know I wasn't a perfect husband. I didn't do this for praise, although she did appreciate it and let me know. I did it because I could see the pattern and I decided if it was inevitable, I would participate in the inevitability of it. My actions were driven by the invasion of beliefs which fit right into my self-image. Vicki was determined that we would finish what we started, without delay. We wouldn't go to bed with dirty dishes and we wouldn't ruin the memory of the party by languishing over stale remnants.

I thought I wanted God to finish what He started in me, but I could not understand the need for me to be *broken* to accomplish it. After all, God was sovereign and He could fix anything. I was irritated with God because I couldn't accept the counterintuitive nature of His ways or understand this path of explosive encounters he had planned for my life. I wanted Him to show me His plan, to point the way and let me cut my way through the brush to get there. I wanted to 'get busy' working on things and quit wasting time.

For some reason, God simply will not be rushed. He is stubborn, just like Vicki. He takes the time to pick up everything that is out of place and thoroughly clean every instrument, preparing it for His purpose. He doesn't rush. He isn't looking past the moment toward another 'mission' as I did looking past my guests to clean up the room.

How could I ever learn to relate to a God whose nature was so opposite to my own? Tell me: why shouldn't I be able to make a difference by my striving?

Look, God... I am a capable ally. I am a proven warrior. I am a finisher. You can use me. Look how strong I am.

The depth of my depravity goes far deeper than I imagined. Father God, you brought me to this place and you orchestrated it with more precision than I ever imagined. I don't know what your plans are but I do know this:

You can rebuild the foundation of my beliefs. You can make me the man you created me to be.

Finish what you started in me, Lord.

2-28-15 Journaling in Prison: The Measure of Brokenness

Why does it seem, Lord, that the nature of business—and even of the church—is tainted by the measurement of human accomplishments or failures? I never saw it before, but now I see that many indelible marks are placed on us, depending on our area of defeat, addiction, deception or etc.

Levels of trust or status are doled out, often based on those who have best concealed their sin or kept it quiet, perhaps while it was being overcome by Your Grace. Now I have to deal with this as I struggle against my desire to conceal my failures.

Paul says he will GLORY in his weakness. How am I supposed to try to hide the Glory of Your power, overcoming my weakness and failures? Yet I want to hide those victories over sin because I know the nature of human judgement and the impact of our failure and sin on our 'status' in the eyes of others. Especially the church.

Why have I been so satisfied for so long in my ability to extol my performance more than Your Grace, and take pride in my efforts more than the Glory of your power in my WEAKNESS?

Help me, Lord, because I don't want to expose myself. Is that my nature or pride or what? Is it ok? Show me, Lord.

My family is at risk if I expose myself, but aren't they and all my brothers and sisters in Christ even more at risk if I deny your power to overcome overwhelming failure and sin?

Is this true for me, Lord?   Am I too busy building my 'alibi,' my excuses, my 'story,' to be willing to be BROKEN before men?   If I am perceived to be 'in-tact' then I fear I may be limiting your Glory, Lord.   Show me what this means. Let me be bare, broken and naked before you, for your Glory. Nothing held back.

Chapter Twelve: Why Am I Here?

"Therefore we do not lose heart. Though outwardly we are wasting away, yet inwardly we are being renewed day by day. For our light and momentary troubles are achieving for us an eternal glory that far outweighs them all. So we fix our eyes not on what is seen, but what is unseen, since what is seen is temporary, but what is unseen is eternal." (2 Cor 4: 16-18 NIV)

Have you ever asked God "WHY"? Why is it that nothing ever turns out like you thought it would? Why does chaos play such a big role in our lives? Why do lessons learned always seem more like punishments endured? Why does ice cream taste so good when it's really so bad for you? (I just threw that last one in there because I'm having a late night craving.)

Doesn't it seem like much of life is a 'bait and switch' scheme? We think we're getting what we bargained for, and then we get the old switch-a-roo. We play the game using our logic and assumptions. We get paid with emotional baggage and mind games. Shouldn't that tell us something?

Back in the early 2000s, I was flying all over the place, doing business everywhere I could. Opportunity seemed to be everywhere, if you had some capital. What a rush. After a great deal of communication, I set aside my trepidation and scheduled a trip to Kiev, Ukraine. I was being offered what seemed like unprecedented access to potential business.

As a western businessman, I brushed aside tales of the previous decade of failed business by westerners in Eastern Europe. I was certain I had discernment (I'm special, intuitive and bullet proof, remember?), that would take me past the blindness of typical westerners in Eastern European countries. We flew a private jet into the country and were escorted with pomp and regalia through customs with relative ease. I brought my own translator, and although the Russian language seemed harsh and angry, he assured me that we were being treated with the utmost respect.

Private cars were waiting to take us to the hotel. I was staying in a suite that occupied the entire top floor. It had its own entertaining areas and conference room. I had to admit, the status afforded to me was quite impressive. People stood ready to do anything I asked. A line of appointments was scheduled for the next several days.

One of the companies I was scheduled to meet with was of particular interest to me. Without their involvement and lavish invitation to cover all of my expenses, I wouldn't have made the trip. Their specific agenda was reserved for a face-to-face meeting, but the overtures were clear. I was very, very interested to partner with them. They were a world-renowned corporation and some of my contacts in the United States were very interested in opening business relations with them.

If I could make the right introductions, I could carve out a great deal of money for myself. I would open the door to the first right of refusal on several fronts if the agreements were handled correctly. We had circulated several drafts of my expectations and theirs. We seemed to be in agreement and an LOI (Letter of Intent) with Non-Disclosure and Non-Compete were put into place.

I felt as if I were in a zoo, the animal on display as an army of representatives filed into the conference room. Refreshments were everywhere and the air was filled with smoke. After a brief exchange of pleasantries, we were engaged in the initial attempts to 'define' the business at hand.

I wondered at times if my translator simply had no real grasp of business nomenclature, or if I was not getting the full story. We seemed to be traveling down a road toward funding an unrelated business with no related purpose. I nodded as I listened, but wondered where the conversation was headed. Perhaps it was more complex than I had initially imagined.

Suddenly, everyone stood. Except me, of course, as I looked around the room confused. Apparently, we were heading to their bank to discuss this relationship behind closed doors. Obediently, I followed, and was loaded in a long line of chauffeured vehicles and raced with our group across the city of Kiev. During the ride, I questioned my translator and attempted to piece together what I might have missed. He seemed clueless as well.

We pulled up to a massive building, ornate with history and obvious governmental significance. I followed as the group nearly ran up the long stairs. Searches, scans and questions were required to enter the building, and it made me uncomfortable. I had no idea why we were there. As an American in a faraway land, I began to wonder if I really had any rights and what they were. I was ushered into a room which appeared to be literally overlaid in gold.

I was offered a seat at the head of the conference table. A new group of men in suits filed into the room, while most of our group was left standing. I was in the Central Bank of the Ukraine. I had read only that morning in the newspaper of intense meetings between Ukraine and Russia over natural gas purchases. Ukraine, according to the papers, owed Russia based Gazprom over 2 billion dollars. They were trying to figure out how to supply their ongoing needs in the wake of this unrest. Winter was nearly upon them. Somehow, I was in the middle of the discussions.

What ensued was a whirlwind of very interesting heated debate. I had no hope of keeping up with the conversation. I was handed a file containing (in English) a series of diagrams. I began to grasp the 'scheme' (not a negative term in Europe, as it is in the U.S.), they believed could bring an agreement. It was a carefully tailored plan defining my role as a mediator, perhaps even a trustee in the process. It was designed to hold pledged assets through Swiss banks and ensure the fulfillment of an agreement between parties who had very little trust in each other.

How is it possible that I was sitting in that room, that day? There had to be thousands of more qualified people to assist in such a transaction. My senses went numb as I stared at the diagrams laying before me. The conversation had resumed and I found myself nearly daydreaming as I looked across the spectacular room.

Then it happened. The far wall seemed to become transparent. I could see the kingdom of heaven watching on the other side. Without words, I understood something powerful. In that moment, it was a vision of reality which stopped time and nearly stopped my heart. The words formed in my thoughts. *I know why I came... But WHY am I here?*

Completing this story would itself make an interesting book, but the most important thing I learned from that day was clear. I knew why I flew to the Ukraine and to Switzerland. I knew why I purposed to schedule the meeting. It didn't take long to realize that the purpose I had for all of the expense and effort to be there, was *not* why I was there.

All of the calculations and anticipations that had brought me to the table were gone. In the midst of the unknown, God had rolled back the curtains and reminded me of His presence. "Greg, your life will be full of times when you 'think' you know why you came. But always remember that I know why you are really here."

This was one of the most powerful moments in my life. I felt God's presence vividly. Even with that revelation, however, most of my life has been lived believing I knew what God was doing. Now, I stared out the window in my prison cell. I knew God was at work but I had no idea what He was up to. I knew why I had come but I didn't know why I was there.

Let's be honest. Haven't we all deceived ourselves with the hidden motives and agendas of our lives? Don't we still expect God to work everything out for our own 'good'?

We expect God to act in a rational, explainable manner and to live up to our expectations so we can explain (logically, of course) why we are His followers and offer up proof that we are justified in our choice.

After all, it is *our* choice, isn't it?

As a western Christian businessman in particular, I had certain expectations. I found it completely beyond imagination that 'a loving God' would design a path which doesn't seem 'loving' at all. After all, I know why I came.

I came to God because I believe He wants the best for me and will part the seas, calm the storms and heal my sickness. I came, obviously, at great personal expense and with careful calculations about my reasons for making this journey to God. I expect that decision will lead to a healthy, prosperous and happy life that *all* makes sense.

I didn't come for unanswered questions. I came for purification of soul and spirit, not for testing and trial in my everyday life. I came because God is my rock, my fortress, my shelter in times of trouble. I came so that through HIS brokenness I could remain UNBROKEN.

I know why I came... But why am I here?

I want to be a marathon runner but I don't want the training. I want to be patient, strong and wise, but I prefer to do it theoretically. I observe the brutality of nature and the punishing lives of our ancestral pioneers, but I do so from a safe distance. I celebrate the endurance of past heroes, but I pray God would protect me from anything that remotely resembles suffering.

Let the potter make something good out of what I already am so that I will never be truly broken.

8-14-14 Journaling From Prison

How was this hidden from me? Why did I not see what was all around me? It's as if the veil has been lifted and the scales have fallen off of my eyes. The sparkling of the razor wire perhaps broke the spell of the prison I had been living in, before I actually came to prison.

What is this drive that burns within me to become something more than I am, as if it were possible? How did I fail to see what I am and what I have? I exchanged it for the pursuit of something I could never catch.

I encapsulated myself in a world of my own making with the belief that I had actually improved my life. Only when those barnacles were painfully removed could I experience what I could never have achieved. Not a destination or an accomplishment, but a state of being. A God-given state of luxury that was given to me, but not activated until I was shocked into comprehension that what I already had through Christ was more than I could ever accumulate myself.

My Secret Identity

I was sure I had chosen my own identity. It was *who* I was; the way I was made. I began to accumulate baggage around me to support my belief in that 'chosen' identity. Each desire, each defense, each obsession required its own combination of supporting roles. These were truth for me, and everything about life was viewed in the background of my identity.

The circumstances and decisions of life took into consideration the needs of my identity and my baggage. It ruled my view of life's basic needs, even of my spiritual needs. They all came into focus based on the myopic perspective of my (largely circumstantial) beliefs. The very definition of life was grafted onto the growing vines of my perspective.

My need for God himself was both to keep my identity from evil, and to bless the woven needs which defined me. I had a never-ending reasoning process in defense of my own identity; an identity that I believed was accurate and in line with the person I was created to be. I was unable to meet anyone, even God, unless they came to me in my own chosen reality.

Yes, I just checked and I am great. I feel sorry for everyone else. Thank you very much.

The Prison I Built For Myself

So, exactly when did prison begin for me? How many years was I 'locked up?' A very good question. Looking back, I try to remember being free. When did I start wrapping scraps of identity around me, covering myself with the shreds of truth I found lying about? I guess we've been sewing fig leaves to cover ourselves for a very long time.

As a child, I clung to the comfort of an identity I could be compatible with. I listened as others defined me. I tried to reject undesirable input.

He's so smart. He figures things out so quickly for his age. He really can sing for a little guy. You can do anything you want in life. (Thank you for that one, Mom.)

Then came the battering ram of my own thoughts. *You'll never be as good as your brother. People don't like you. You're not popular like some of the other kids. You are different.*

The belief system adapts. The self-talk chisels away. The tender spots get calloused. The bullet-proof 'era' begins, and everything I surround myself with is consistent with my identity. My prison sentence has begun.

I may not have been confined physically, but I was never free. In the crisis of my beliefs, I prayed desperately for God to defend my domain. Thank you, Lord, for setting me free. Thank you, Lord, for loving me enough to rinse it all away.

I know why I am here. My freedom began just before my incarceration. It was only possible through the devastating release from the prison I had built for myself. Until that identity died, I would never be truly free.

My life of freedom began when I was broken.

8-7-14 Journaling From Prison

Good morning, Lord. Your presence is everywhere and your love gives me breath this morning. Speak to me in ways only you can. Open my mind and eyes to all that you are and want to be in me. Let me make you proud of me. Your thoughts, your purpose, your way. Lord, I miss my home and my family. I miss the blessings you gave me, which I took for granted. Let me finish this path in your strength, for I have none of my own. Be my shelter and sanctuary. Be my ever-present help in time of need.

I am not losing this time. I am spending it with you. You are my source and strength. I am learning complete dependence on you. Help me to hear your voice and believe, even when I do not see the outcomes.

Do you have a place and plan for me after all my failures? Is it possible for me to stand firm in faith when the tendency I now have is uncertainty, especially in this place?   Let me be one of the men who hears your voice, my Lord.

I am dust.   My aspirations are invaded with the clear knowledge that they are meaningless without your infusion of life, presence and blessing.   Release me from my own thoughts and bring me into your story as you see fit.   In this place, I realize even more clearly how futile my own efforts are.

When I think of 'doing,' I don't know the way.   I can only be what you are in me.   All of the things I have felt so capable of, lay before me and are meaningless self-deception.

I can do all things only through Christ, who strengthens me. You, my Lord, are strength and my only source of redemption.   Your purpose for me is to walk in your ways, to be faithful and serve you with gladness.   Lord, I believe in the calm strength that comes by your hand.   Release me into the current of your Spirits Power.

Chapter Thirteen: Finding My Place In This World

So, here I am. I'm in prison. I lay awake at night, staring at the too-close ceiling. My mind races, sorting its way through my past as if my next stop was a confessional. Many of those scenes I never wanted to replay.

God, forgive me. I had forgotten about that. It didn't seem so bad at the time, but now I see the disgusting agony of it. I never want to be that man again.

Is this my destiny? Have I filled the crevices of my mind with so many meaningless things that I am doomed to be tortured by them? Am I forever helpless to restore the relationships I've destroyed, or will I be forgiven by those I've wronged?

I am alone, now more than ever. Isolated from love and friendship, I resist depression and self-debasement. Silently, I search for a thread of meaning I can rebuild on. I only find one which will hold.

While it's impossible to adequately share the experience of prison, I found that the thread of God's love, even as a fine, invisible line, was enough to support me. I learned to trust it.

Redefining the foundation of my life was not on my agenda. I didn't even believe it was possible. I only wanted to get this experience behind me, yet I found the paradigm of faith there. Displaced from everything and everyone in my life, I finally found my place in this world.

The TV Room

It seems God's Word is constantly unveiling paradoxes related to our position of hierarchy in the Kingdom of God: glory in our weakness, the first shall become last, he who would be first in the kingdom must be the servant of all, do unto others as you would have them do unto you, unless a seed goes into the ground and dies it won't produce anything. Live and let die.

Ok, maybe not that last one, but I kinda like it.

Everything in prison has its own set of rules. Most of it was defined through years of tradition, both relayed and enforced by the inmates. The TV room was no exception.

There were approximately one hundred inmates who used the TV room our wing shared. The room, filled completely with chairs, would hold about fifty (so long as everyone was close enough to tell who had showered).

Every spot, even if it appeared to be empty, belonged to someone; nobody took someone else's spot. With not much else to do, TV is treasured in prison.

Then comes football season, and the tiny space becomes jammed with people looking in from every doorway. The noise of it was overwhelming. The smell of it was often more overwhelming. Try to imagine watching a football game on a tiny screen, with 50 guys screaming at the TV. Yeah, it was pretty amazing. Last night, I watched my first pre-season game at home and I had flashbacks. I couldn't stop thanking God that I was watching from home.

The TV room protocols were a bit concerning when I first arrived. I was informed that in order to actually have a spot in the TV room, someone either has to leave or you have to buy the spot. The waiting list for people leaving was pretty well developed. I didn't really know anyone yet, so for the first 3 months, I just didn't use the TV room. Buying a seat was an entirely new concept as well, since nobody actually had any money. The economy of prison was extremely interesting and efficient. A topic for another day.

Sometimes I stopped in the hallway to read the CNN ticker or scan a ballgame. Overall, I felt out of place. It was a domain I didn't belong in. Then, one day, standing in the hallway, another inmate asked me if I wanted to use his chair. Awkwardly, I nodded. I was in.

There were four TVs with a (very inmate-defined) list of shows that would be played. With a radio and earbuds, you tuned to the appropriate channel for audio. I never touched a remote. Gradually, I found people who didn't watch sports or who didn't watch on Mondays, etc. I found the spots I was interested in and bounced around with my new 'buddies.' In fact, they were excited to be able to accommodate me, and some even went out of their way to make sure I was taken care of. Then it happened. One of my cellies (cellmates) moved to a wing on the other side of the facility. Guess what. I inherited his chair.

At last. My own SPOT.

What is it about carving out our own territory that matters so much to us? I go to church and I sit in essentially the same place every week. In prison, I had my spot in the cafeteria where I sat 90% of the time, and everyone knew it. I was really irritated when someone grabbed my spot. When I go to a movie, I have a spot I like to sit. When we eat around the family table, sit on the deck or in the living room, I have my spot. Now, I even have a spot in the TV room in prison.

I'm not comfortable just going with the flow. I want to have a plan. If you're going to do something, it should have a technique, a process, a method.

Then, there's this idea of God's Will and purpose. Does it make sense that God's purpose for us is to wait, to relax, to listen and be quiet? Sounds more like a yoga class or a meditation exercise, which is not my style. I see God as a warrior, crashing the gates, battling to take territory and being constantly diligent against the assault of the enemy. Yes, that's the God I know; a God of *action*.

Yet, here I am, a guy who has 'tried' to seek God's will and to do something important (FOR GOD, of course). I have worked hard, 'strived for the right... willing to march into hell for a heavenly cause.' (Ok, I'm looking for the theme song from Don Quixote or the Patriot here).

I'm in Prison. A guy who is equipped to *strive* and now must wait.

I want to know where I belong. I want to define my methods, my plans, and my space. Now, the definition of my space is a 10x10 block room I share with three other guys, or a single plastic chair in the TV room. A top bunk and a uniform with no simulation of productivity anywhere in sight.

I feel like a racehorse locked in a stall; a Lamborghini pulling a wagon. This was not at all what I signed up for; not at all who I believe I am. The compartmental life I so carefully built does not make room for this reality.

Teach me Lord. Teach me, Lord... To wait?

The beat goes on... Without me.

9-12-14 Journaling From Prison

How can it be that I alone believe that I must carry or work or persevere in order to see the fulfillment of my life? How did I fall into such nonsense? Is it ego and pride that caused me to believe that somehow God and others needed my strength and my actions in order to be blessed? Is that, in itself, blasphemy? Forgive me, Lord.

I exalt myself by my own actions and the actions of my past. I put my head down and strain over the blessings that YOU alone have given. I give token acknowledgment that you have blessed primarily by acknowledging your presence in me.

It makes me nauseated to think about my failures now, especially in this place. I see your greatest work being performed and I am powerless to participate. Forgive me for my arrogance. Forgive me for my belief that I had any strength at all.

You alone know my inheritance in your Kingdom because you ordained it. You alone are unchanging and unbreakable. My life is renewed only by your presence. Of myself, I am utterly ignorant and helpless.

A desperate feeling has somehow merged with a sense of freedom and peace; peace that comes from you through my dependence on you, and freedom that comes from laying down in green pastures because I have no strength to stand.

My fear, my agony, my brokenness... all present as humility and ultimate servanthood to you. Finally, I know what you have always known: I am dust. I am broken. But, I am yours.

Chapter Fourteen: The Compartmentalized Life

'Trust in the Lord with all your heart and lean not on your own understanding; in all your ways submit to him and he will make your paths straight. Do not be wise in your own eyes, fear the lord and shun evil. This will bring health to your body and nourishment to your bones.' (Proverbs 3: 5-8 NIV)

I remember an episode from *Hogan's Heroes* (yes, I'm old). Strangely, in those days, it didn't require vulgarity or vivid violence to engage us (although Helga did, at times, dress a little risqué). Hogan was a prisoner of war in Germany during WWII. He and his men matched wits with the infamous Colonel Klink. They ran an entire IMF operation, every weekly episode out of their barracks. The engineering was amazing.

Back to my point. I remember an episode where a bomb had dropped into the camp but had not exploded. After great stress and a lot of sweat, Hogan stood ready to clip the proverbial wire that would disarm the bomb. Colonel Klink was given the opportunity to choose the black or red wire.

Klink chooses the black wire. Hogan moves toward the black wire and at the last possible second, reaches to clip the red one. The bomb is disarmed. Everyone takes a deep breath and cheers. Klink then asks the obvious question: "I said to clip the black wire?"

Hogan, in wisdom of the ages (and a fabulous era of family based sitcom), calmly says "Well, I didn't know which wire to clip, but I knew one thing for certain."

"What's that?" Klink asks.

Hogan replies: "I knew you would pick the wrong one."

Ever feel that way about your life? I always saw myself as Hogan, not Klink. I always knew which wire to clip and I was always the hero. How did I become the villain? How did I become patient zero in an epidemic that had infected so many? How do I accept the fact that my actions and compulsive beliefs caused other people to suffer?

I have to confess that I struggle to separate the fierceness of my pride from my determination. For me to really 'set my jaw' on something and get it done, there seems to always be a certain prescribed dosage of adrenaline involved. When my adrenaline triggers, it brings with it a comfort zone of ego and the self-determination of my compulsive beliefs. Those are compartments of my life I am very comfortable with. I believed I had the ability to 'come through' because I had spoken it.

It's the counterintuitive truth; a paradox that I have learned to identify, just like Hogan did. It's not about logic, determination, skill or good intentions. I have all of those. It's about where my comfort, strength and understanding come from. It's about the activating beliefs of my identity. Unless my identity is defined in Christ, I'm going to clip the wrong wire.

How can I possibly separate my diligent efforts from the core of my beliefs? How do I get my mind around a world where I don't 'understand' it all for myself? Why is my strength not enough?

The compartmentalized nature of my life does not admit weakness.

I Corinthians 3: 18-20   Do not deceive yourselves.   If any of you think you are wise by the standards of this age, you should become 'fools' so that you may become wise.   For the wisdom of this world is foolishness in Gods sight. As it is written: 'He catches the wise in their craftiness' and again, 'The Lord knows that the thoughts of the wise are futile.'

What Does "Compartmentalization" Mean?

Perhaps I should take a moment to define what I mean by 'compartmentalization.' Pretty sure you will get the idea as you read about my experiences going forward, but it deserves its own moment in the script.

Have you ever talked to the person who doesn't seem to be able to control their language, but who never swears around the 'preacher?' We have a tendency to say, "See, they can control it if they want to," but I take a different view.

Let me tell you how I mastered the use of compartmentalization (and for three 'easy' payments of $9.95, you can too).

As humans, we have the unique ability to build entirely distinct and separate compartments of our lives. They don't even need to intersect with each other. How we act at church is completely different than how we act at the ball game. How we treat our children is completely different in public than it is at home. How we 'react' to certain stimuli is absolutely defined by the 'compartment' of our life we are living in at that moment.

We build them, define them and each has their own comfort level that we can make ourselves at home in. Most are pretty simple, just complying with societal norms. Some can be very private and filled with assumptions we've made. We may only go there by accident, but we have them carefully framed up in a place we keep hidden and separate from where we live day-to-day.

At least, that's how it worked for me.

As time went on, more compartments were built. They helped me make sense out of my life. They prevented the trauma of intersecting realities and thoughts that were not compatible. Compartments of my life had to have the capacity to contain matter and anti-matter, or there was going to be an explosion of unprecedented proportions. Think about it: how else can we explain the experiences we see every day? Affairs where 'apparently' nobody was supposed to get hurt; entirely separate realities which manifest as Dr. Jekyll and Mr. Hyde, who are never present at the same time.

I lived in them and retreated to them based on needs or circumstances. I used them for survival. I used them to justify myself to myself, to others, and even to God. I worked to 'become' what I believed made me acceptable. I clung to this developed persona of compartmentalization. I even carried it into the presence of God as an offering to Him.

I believed in my fragmented sacrifice and I expected God to bless it.

Don't Trust Your Instincts

Isn't that depressing? After all, I took the strengths test, and baby, I have those gifts. I am equipped and I know how to take action. (It feels so right, how could it be wrong?)

Greg, what are you trying to say?

Simply this: our compulsive beliefs have become integrated in us at the very cellular level. Maybe I am overstating this, but I have come to believe one thing for sure. Living by the principles of my own understanding, driven by my own randomly compiled belief system, I will *never* get it right. I believed in God, but I trusted in myself. It seemed completely natural.

Until my instincts become completely controlled by God's Spirit, they can't be trusted. My compartmentalization must be *broken*.

What should I do?

Asking myself that question was like an attorney representing himself. As the story goes, he has a fool for a client. In my broken state, I was forced to make a few observations that were completely contrary to my previous beliefs:

1. My assumptions were wrong. I thought I was more than capable of accomplishing the purpose for my life. I thought my talents and capabilities were more than enough to bring satisfaction.

2. I'm blind. I can't trust my own understanding. It leads to a compartmentalized life of self-justification. I lack the ability to see ten seconds into the future or around the first corner. Anything I get right is probably an accident.

3. I have to quit trying to perform; to make it right. God knows I am dust. The plan I want to fulfill, which gives peace, satisfaction, reconciliation and joy, is beyond my strength or ability.

It's not easy. I hate it. I want to actively fix every bit of damage created by the momentum of my failures, mistakes and sin. It doesn't feel 'okay' to leave them in God's hands. If I'm not taking responsibility for myself, then who is?

This never became real in my life until I was broken. Abundant life had to be more than living an effectively compartmentalized life that seems to 'work.' Somehow, I had to embrace the possibility that God's designed purpose for my life was more than I could ask for or imagine.

God's design was more than the accumulation of my compulsive beliefs. God's purpose for me was a plan of redemptive belief.

1-28-15 - Journaling From Prison

It feels a little ironic writing about a compartmentalized life when I am in prison, but it seems so obvious now. Searching for a restored heart made me realize how inverted my thinking had become.

I am living in the tragedy of my own understanding about life. It wasn't just limited, it was inverted. You tried to show me this in so many ways but I just kept nodding and continuing to swing the mallet, butted up against the rock of Christ but clearly building on the sand.

You are the one who said that the first shall be last and the last shall be first. That the greatest in the kingdom would be the servant of all. Maybe I should have regarded everything with that potential. Lord, how deep does this paradigm go?

I remember when I began the process of building clear compartments. It's too painful to talk about, Lord. You know it all. Resolving it was so painful because to live with it meant drawing conclusions about myself and about my life that left me alone and ashamed. So, I built that first wall. I couldn't stand the endless loop of self-abasement and self-hatred that I felt. I remember it. I was in pain. So, I built that wall, and it worked. The pain stopped. The resources I received from that part of my life seemed easily redirected into areas that I could control. At least, I thought I could control them.

I exchanged that vulnerable area of my life for a business life that welcomed me, embraced me and rewarded me with soothing praise that I had seared off from others. I didn't need anyone. It was an exchange that turned off the pain, even though it reached such proportion that the numbness of my heart couldn't even respond to stimulation of love or pain.

Only you could restore me, Lord. I don't know how you did it, but I remember the out-of-body experience when it all came back together. It couldn't happen with me at the controls. I see that now. It only happened because I was broken.

2-1-15 Journaling From Prison

I suppose, because I was so compartmentalized in my life, I saw you that way too, Lord. It seems to me that most of the people I know see you only through one channel as well. They see you as judge or as Father, or perhaps only relate to you on one level. Everything we know about life or about salvation seems to be interpreted only through whatever funnel or filter we use when we think about you.

I know we all start somewhere with you, and hopefully walk into more maturity, but I know you are not interpreted ONLY by where I am at the moment. You are everything. You are all of those interpretations at once. All of the things I have never yet experienced and more. How is that possible? How do I learn to see you far beyond the scope of my understanding?

Here in prison, I am amazed by the people who seek you but only want you in one area of their lives. Help me not to fall into that trap. I don't want my life and my relationship with you to be built on the bunker of safety alone, or in a view of my own life that begins another process of fortification and compartmentalization to make me feel secure. I have had enough of that way of living.

Now, I suddenly realize that this is more about me trying to compartmentalize YOU than it is to compartmentalize myself. I don't want to define you. I don't want to limit my willingness to see you in every situation. I don't want to cling to a particular view that traps me in a fundamental or experiential relationship with you.

I cling to Your Grace, but I still want to perform. I still want to please you, even in my weakness and brokenness. I can't seem to help it.

Forgive me for trying to cling to my birth right as your child and straining to build my life on my compartmentalized image of you, God. I see now that you were not going to let that image survive. You knew I had to be broken down. I had to let go.

I never imagined I could walk down this road. I feel so bombarded with unworthiness and doubt. All of the ways I kept my faith in-tact in the past were based on my old habits of compartmentalizing it in my life.

I never imagined that you could manifest yourself in so many ways, all at once. The Lord God of Angel Armies, and yet my boyhood friend as well. You meet my needs even beyond salvation. You let me see how un-compartmentalized and un-fragmented YOU ARE, giving me hope that I could be that way too.

My instinct to compartmentalize was very real. It came from a desire to understand, to protect, and to control. It managed my fear when the only way to let go of fear was in the expanse of trusting God; the counterintuitive idea of trusting what I cannot control.

'Trust in the Lord and do good; dwell in the land and enjoy safe pasture. Take delight in the Lord; trust in him and he will do this; he will make your righteous reward shine like the dawn. Your vindication like the noonday sun. Be still before the Lord and wait patiently for him....' (Psalms 37: 3-7 NIV)

It's not natural. I know that. I could never have made this decision on my own because I was leaning on my own self-constructed reality. God cracked open the compartments of my own making and gave me a chance to let the abundant life come in. Thank you, Lord. You heard the cry of my heart and set me free from my compartmentalized life.

Chapter Fifteen: Disqualified

'For you, God, tested us; you refined us like silver. You brought us into prison and laid burdens on our backs. You let people ride over our heads; we went through fire and water, but you have brought us to a place of abundance.' (Psalm 66: 10-12 NIV)

I knew the call was coming, but it still caught me off guard. Why do we hold on to what is so temporary? Why do we cling to shreds of sentiment in a world where only the practical and logical seem to survive?

"Greg, you probably know why I'm calling." It was the district superintendent for our denomination. We were friends of sorts, and had known each other for a long time. He had observed my life, knew my best and worst, but we never talked about it. It seems, especially in the church, it is practically forbidden to discuss our sins, as ironic as that may be.

"There are people who believe you should no longer participate in an active role in our music program, Greg. I'm calling to ask you not to sing this Sunday." Even I was no longer comfortable in that position, but it seemed like the only thing I had left.

More than a year after my indictment, our worship pastor had gone out of his way to pull me into the program. He knew my situation. Before consenting, I asked him to do his 'due diligence' and make certain there were no objections. I knew in my heart it would eventually end badly, but he insisted I participate. And I desperately wanted to belong.

Another year had passed before the call came. I kicked myself for believing everything was alright. I assured him he did not need to worry about offending me. "I don't disagree at all. I love the church and I don't want to be a distraction in any way." The conversation was over. Secretly, I felt the numbness of another gut punch. I wished he had been calling to offer his support and prayers, but I knew his job was much more difficult than most.

For several decades as a businessman (and a donor), I was asked to serve on boards. I was involved in special committees, given awards and invited to special events. I like to believe I gave sound advice from bank boards, to university boards, to hospital boards, to church boards and charities. All of this occurred because I had achieved a degree of success and status.

Of course, if you've been involved in such things, you also know how it works. Influence and the ability to contribute might be the true motivation for your involvement. People want to surround themselves (as I did) with successful people; people untarnished by failure, who raise the standard, are respectable and trustworthy.

The church is no different. It's God (alone) who forgives, God who justifies, God who demonstrates grace and mercy. The measure of man will always be in conflict with the measure of God. Mankind wants a hero, just as the Israelites wanted a king. So, we struggle to maintain our own persona and defend our weakness. It's too dangerous to expose ourselves. It's human nature, and quite frankly I am not here to debunk that paradigm.

As a broken man, I find a bit of irony in my own experiences. It isn't my intent to create any 'shock and awe.' I had simply never been the guy on the outside looking in. As long as I was able to keep the facade of my own identity in tact (at all costs), I was accepted. Being vulnerable would have isolated me. Yes, the church is full of hypocrites—the greatest paradox of all.

Simultaneously saint and sinner, every one of us.

8-13-14 Journaling From Prison

Lord, my weakness overwhelms me. When I see the weariness of my life and my pathetic struggle, it makes me sick. My pseudo-strength is laughable. My need goes far beyond my strength.

I believe in your ability to heal and restore. I believe in your constant drawing of me to yourself. You are pulling me out of any comfort that ever existed so that I may fully rest in you (I pray).

I have nothing to offer except what you yourself are able to do with this broken vessel. What you have made is for your purpose and can never be rendered useless. Thank you, Lord.

I used to hire machinists in our business. Reviewing their applications, I found good education, impressive recommendations and work history. Unfortunately, most had very little experience beyond production. The procedures of a true tool maker are rigorous and defined by one primary perspective: you must be able to imagine everything that can go wrong. Then, your procedures have to prevent them. That is the mark of skill and maturity in a tool maker.

Most of the tools, molds, and dies we worked on were elaborate. You could wrap up hundreds of hours on a single section. Tolerances were tight. Even the slightest unanticipated stress in the metal could scrap out a tool, already worth thousands of dollars. I didn't want any of my guys making those kinds of mistakes.

The only way to anticipate what can go wrong on a job is through experience: the sound of something going wrong, the way a cutter looks or sounds in the cut, the color of the chips or the characteristics of an electrode, the way a part is clamped or any stresses that might result. In other words, the only way you can succeed on my job is because you have scrapped out a lot of other jobs in the past.

Working with less experienced machinists, I tried to prevent potential mistakes. I described the process in great detail. I attempted to take out the variables. Unfortunately, no matter how sincere the listener, there is no substitute for experience.

I find myself waking to the lyric of old hymns I knew as a child. I am amazed by the wisdom. I hear generations of experience, now that I have 'crossed over' to their perspective. I sang them, but I had never really known them through the pain of personal experience.

Living With My Head in the Clouds

As a very young pilot, I was eager to go further in my training. I wanted my instrument rating. I wanted to fly in the clouds. I didn't want to be restricted by visibility or by weather. I knew the next step was to get my instrument ticket. Not wanting to be restricted by having my instrument license is tantamount to saying you want to be in business for yourself so you can work less hours. I didn't see that yet.

I remember talking about flying with a veteran pilot at our local airport on a clear, beautiful day. He said something I will never forget. I was lamenting I didn't have time to go 'up.' He looked into the sky and paused as if reminiscing. "It's a lot better to be down here wishing you were up there than up there wishing you were down here."

I never forgot that, even though I had not experienced it yet. Once I did, my entire perspective changed. Adventure, excitement and pleasure-seeking gave way to experience. I was determined to be the best pilot I could be. I wanted to be familiar with those conditions so that I could stay out of them.

As a machinist and as a pilot, I'm much more aware of the things I don't know. I don't know what's in that cloud, no matter how friendly it looks. Pilots share this information with critical reporting called PIREPS. Pilot reports. We hear about what other people have experienced and we rely on their willingness to tell their stories. We learn from their experiences and their mistakes.

I value the pilot who has gone through those conditions. Theory is nothing compared to reality. There are a lot of armchair quarterbacks, even among aviators. What if you could train with an instructor who has thousands of hours in military aircraft or 20 years of commercial flying experience? Maybe he's even walked away from a mistake that destroyed the airplane.

Does failure make someone less qualified or more qualified? Have you ever asked yourself this question? Does your ability to conceal your brokenness make you more desirable or less desirable? It's really quite a paradox.

Would you agree that society (as a whole) rewards those who are able to conceal their brokenness? Don't we encourage people to maintain an identity which denies weakness and failure? Can we truly know God without brokenness?

I can't see what is inside the cloud in front of me. I can't always avoid the weather of life. The buffer in my personal and business lives seemed real and powerful. However, it was no match for the unknown. Defending my 'identity' caused me to crash.

Have you ever felt that type of conflict? Has anything ever slapped you so hard that you had to question your own beliefs?

God had other plans for me. He released me from the identity of the role I had built for myself. That experience of freedom transcended anything I had ever understood before.

Theoretical became experiential. My disqualification became my only qualification. Brokenness gave way to renewal.

This is my PIREP to you.

8-6-14 Journaling From Prison

I love you, My Lord. I read in your word about Joseph and how, through him, you blessed others. That is so exciting. Let my service to you be like that. blessing others through your word and your touch. He spent years unjustly as a slave and in prison, then you raised him up for your purpose. Perhaps his time in prison also helped purify him and prepare him for your service. None of these things would have happened if you had not changed the direction of their lives.

Let me join the ranks of men serving you; men who were purified by fire and became your instruments. They could do nothing of themselves, only what you revealed to them. They trusted you in all these things to deliver them.

Praise your name, my Holy Father, for your patience and never-tiring offer to show me what you are all about. You could easily be numb to me after the thousands of years of watching humans walk against your ways, but you are not.

You have open arms to me beyond what I can understand. Thank you, Lord. Let my thoughts and actions be rooted only in you. Purify me by the fire of your presence through love and mercy. May my entire life resonate your authority over me.

2-2-15 Journaling From Prison

You showed me this morning that when I prayed the prayer "I want to be who you created me to be," I was thinking about all kinds of things in life, career and actions. Now you've shown me that 'being who I was created to be' was all about being in a relationship with you; experiencing the glory you intended to focus in me and living life in your joy and anticipation.

You had been waiting to clear the cobwebs of my existence to show me what living is all about. It's not about 'doing,' but about embracing your love relationship.

Thank you, Lord. Let's keep taking it higher and closer, and preparing for more of you in me. I don't really know what that means, but I want to know how to love you more. I am so excited.

Chapter Sixteen: The Ultimate Irony

'Wait for the Lord; be strong and take heart and wait for the Lord.' (Psalm 27: 14 NIV)

Times flies so quickly, especially when you're busy attacking a project. I have always enjoyed a sense of accomplishment. It has its own euphoria.

Prison isn't like that. The thing I worked so hard to avoid could not be avoided in prison: unoccupied time. It was a sentence worse than death for me. When I stepped into that place, time came to a grinding halt. The sense of urgency vanished.

Of course, I had made plans of all the things I could accomplish during this time. I'm a planner. I joked it was a monastery I could rest up in. That makes about as much sense as the old pain reliever commercial: "I haven't got time for the pain." Saturday Night Live did a play about this commercial, which showed people who finally had time for the pain. Just as crazy.

There was nothing more painful for me than too much time to think; too much time to run endless circles around my failures, my mistakes, and my sin. I remember the first few days up at 5am, getting dressed, making my bed and having breakfast at 6am. Since it was summer, I went outside for a walk. I admired the beauty of the sun as it glistened on the razor wire at the medium security prison just down the hill. Ah yes, the beauty of nature.

In prison, the only thing actually required on your schedule is 'count time.' As a new arrival, I didn't even have a uniform yet, much less a watch. Suddenly I realized that the track I was walking was empty, and I was at the farthest point from the building. Then I heard the announcement: "Recreation is closed. Report to your assigned area for census." The shoes I was issued were in terrible condition. Now terrified, I ran toward the entrance to face the C.O.'s glare as he blocked my path.

After census, I returned to the track with a book. I kept an eye out to see what everyone else was doing because I was sure it must be about time for lunch. Finally, I asked someone what time it was. About 9:30am. I had done everything I could imagine doing in a day, and it was only 9:30. I went back to my cell and wondered what I would do for the rest of the day. It occurred to me that if I brushed my teeth again, I could probably burn another ten minutes.

Something had to change. All my life, I engineered circumstances to change around me. Now, if there was going to be change, it would have to be in me.

I am adaptable, but I would never have described myself as 'conforming.' Within a week of my incarceration I remember Marty, one of my cellies, telling me "You need to stop trying to make sense of things, it will just drive you crazy."

I want to be careful making any sweeping judgments about government-run agencies. There were some good people in the institution who tried to make the best of it. Some even treated us as actual 'people.' What is unique about government agencies is the level of mind-numbing bureaucracy. I believe a lot of good workers gradually became as institutionalized as the inmates.

The government apparently believes what is needed is more laws. Citizens would not know when to use the restroom if not told to do so. In the world of government oversight, prison pretty much tops the list. Can you imagine living in an institution run by the

118

DMV or the IRS? That flicker of recognition you felt is the best I can do.

The entire process from indictment to incarceration is built on a very important premise you need to understand: they can break the rules; you can't. If they are in error, it was just a mistake. If you make a mistake in prison, no matter how small, it is clearly intentional and punishable.

Fear in prison is very real. They can dictate the very direction of your life. They can put you in handcuffs, put you in the hole or ship you to another institution. They can add additional time of deprivation to your life.

You may think I'm talking about issues like fighting or drugs or blatant disobedience to an officer. That happens, but I'm also talking about taking a green banana out of the cafeteria. By tomorrow it might be ripe, but you have to run a covert operation to accomplish it. Who knew it was criminal to use an old peanut butter jar to keep food from soaking up the taste of laundry detergent in your locker? Everything must be kept in its original container, apparently.

The list of things considered punishable (inside) is endless. You have to become a criminal and learn to hide things. A new rule might be made up next week. Keeping the inmates off balance seemed necessary. Keeping the level of drama high kept anyone from becoming comfortable. This is prison, you're not supposed to feel at home.

Any programs to help each other or to rehabilitate were initiated by the inmates themselves. Often, we had to conceal them like an underground church in China. We started a program to collect basic toiletries for new guys coming in. We provided them essentials they would not have yet. We had to hide it because it was against the rules to give another inmate anything of value.

Bible studies, classes taught by the inmates, mentoring and tutoring were all self-directed. With exception of the chaplain, it seemed the actual staff was focused on tearing people down. Everything was followed by a threat or confiscation.

The washing machine is not working after being used by 100 guys night and day for the past two years. "You guys broke it. We have one down in maintenance, but we're going to teach you a lesson. You have to do without it for a week."

I had time to reflect on how I had dealt with business and employees. Hundreds of people depended on me. I'm sure I handed down edicts I thought made sense and they didn't understand. They could not have known the reasoning behind our decisions or policies. They probably thought I sat around thinking of ways to make their lives more difficult. I probably demanded things that seemed crazy to the people on the front lines.

I have 'authority,' so I must be smarter, right? Watching human beings relegated to pointless tasks made me realize I had done the same. I had human resources that were un-deployed in my business and I was oblivious. I assumed I was supposed to have all the answers. I was wrong.

Isn't God patient with us? A book could be written on the nonsense of prison life. Probably a hundred books could be written on the nonsense of the life I had been living. I thought I was smarter than God.

Did I say that out loud?

I saw God as a resource manual or a reference guide, perhaps even an option in the list of 'best practices' in my peer group. Since I didn't hear Him barking orders, I assumed He was waiting for me to make decisions. He would give me the 'thumbs up' if He agreed.

Like Pavlov's dogs, I figured if God blessed me He approved of my actions. I threw out prayers for wisdom and blessing. Pretty cool how that worked out for me. I didn't realize I was living out the ultimate irony of life. It took prison for me to understand freedom.

3-10-15 Journaling in Prison

I don't know where it all started to go wrong. Where I began to segment the truth from 'my truth.' Where I ate the forbidden fruit. Where I began to actually craft, design and believe the lies. Lies of convenience, of image, of persuasion, of fierce conviction. Where I started believing my own press. Where I started believing the praise and reliance of others.

Was it really 'the evil one,' or was it simply the chiseling of a reality as I wanted it to be? I was so good at it. The compartments of my life so air-tight and secure that they never overlapped... Well almost never... How DID I begin to lose trust in what was so natural?

Thank you, Father, for showing me your unconditional love through your discipline. You gathered me in your arms once all the plates had crashed. You showed me the most incredible blessing in all our existence. Your intimate, passionate, unending love and mercy. That, by Your Grace, I could be one with you, through the completed work of Jesus Christ, my Lord.

Imagine being the driver in a car and being the only one who doesn't know where they're going. Everyone is giving you directions and you're the clueless one at the wheel.

When you look back on your life, how many times do you think you really knew where you were going? We think we have it all together and we know the rules. We think we know where we're going and how to get there. We *think* we know what is best for us.

How can we really know? All we know is what we want, what we think, and what we extrapolate from the inputs we have available. Perhaps we even believe that God has the 'obligation' to tell us where we are going.

Maybe you have a destination in mind, but at every turn you simply take the lane with the least cars in it. You turn whichever direction seems easiest at the time. If the arrow's green, you follow it. Do you think you will ever arrive at your destination?

Hey, it's an open door; a good deal, a great opportunity, a windfall. Let's do that. We'll make money and we'll be happy, but no matter how good things look, we have *no idea* what is *really* behind Door Number 3. It looks glamorous. The crowd is screaming for me to pick it. It's exciting, but *how* can I know for sure?

I actually believe that God cares about me and that He already knows what is behind Door Number 3. Not only does He know, but He knows the impact and implications it will have on my life and the lives of others. I believe He has an active plan and purpose for me.

I Accidentally Got It Right

Late one night, 20 years ago, I was trying to leave the plant. As I finally went to leave, one of our second shift employees waved as he ran my way. Honestly, I was less than thrilled, but I knew my role. I let my impatience be known as I asked what he needed.

Don't you love it when someone interrupts you and says, "Sorry, I don't want to bother you"? (Uh... kinda late, you already are bothering me). Yeah, that was the gear I was driving in at that moment.

It didn't happen all at once, but it happened. It turns out his life was falling apart and he had to talk to someone. He wouldn't stop. I had no real interest in knowing all of these things, but suddenly I knew that God was present.

I don't remember the details. I do remember stopping, speaking a few words to him and laying my hands on him in prayer.

In that moment, a single overwhelming thought came to me: *what if this moment is the very reason I am in business?* What if God brought me to this point so that I could have an impact on a single person, a single family?

This shook my sense of urgency and importance. I have never forgotten it, even though I didn't always know what to do with the thought.

What if the 'new car' was behind Door Number 3 and we missed it? Is it possible that what God knows about Door Number 3 is so far beyond our understanding that we think we got it wrong? Do we think that God doesn't care or isn't paying attention?

We don't know the impact on how our time will be spent. We don't know the impact on the lives we will come into contact with. We don't know the places this decision will cause us to be, and at what times. We don't know the destiny that God has placed into motion and how it will be affected.

If I truly believe in God, then I must trust that *even prison* brings about a plan and purpose that is greater than all my prayers of intercession.

Can God Still Use Me?

A few years ago, a former employee stopped by. I was right in the middle of this time of destruction. I wasn't really interested in opening the door to conversation about my wasted life. I had never operated from such a posture of weakness.

He came by to thank me. I couldn't imagine what for. As the story unfolded, my heart broke. He talked about a conversation I couldn't even remember. He credited that moment as a turning point in his life. From his perspective, I had believed in him when he didn't believe in himself. It meant so much to him that I had listened and seemed to genuinely care.

As he left, the heat of emotion overtook me. I wept uncontrollably. I didn't remember the interaction at all. I'm sure I was focused on something I thought was important at the time. Somehow, God had used me. I probably thought the conversation was insignificant. It turned out to be more significant than anything else I was doing. God was showing me that the most important accomplishments of my life would likely happen when I made room for the things I didn't understand.

I want to make room for what God is doing, no matter what else seems to be going on. Even while I was hanging my head in weakness, my life's purpose was being fulfilled. Today, I am beginning to see the significance of it all.

I wasn't able to see this irony until I was broken.

10-4-14 Journaling From Prison

You are my teacher, Lord. You teach through struggle and you reveal yourself as I pour myself out to you. Your love is seen by the path you lead me down from darkness to light, deception to revelation.

The small exchange in earthly, fleshly perspective is nothing compared to the joy of your coming and the Holy Spirits presence in me. I wake to the stream of the Spirit's thoughts and giving Glory to you, Lord, because that is the theme of the Spirit within me.

I raise my hand in praise and thanks because there is nothing on the earth that could rival the peace and joy of knowing you and sharing life with you. I feel I have been elevated from a position of blindness and struggle to one of light and endless possibilities. My eyes were blind, but now I see the conjoined nature of my existence in spirit and flesh. To fight one, or to be aware of one and not the other, is debilitating and pointless.

I ask now only that my eyes may see and value the urgency and timing and importance that truly exist in your realm.   Amen.

Chapter Seventeen: Comfortable Chairs

'My comfort in my suffering is this: Your promise preserves my life.' (Psalm 119: 50 NIV)

'Even though I walk through the darkest valley, I will fear no evil, for you are with me; your rod and your staff, they comfort me' (Psalm 23: 4 NIV)

I am a master at taking things for granted. I never even noticed my little toe until I caught it on the edge of the nightstand in the darkness. How does that little message travel all the way to my brain and commandeer everything? We should have the ability to hit the snooze button or something, right?

By and large, if something isn't screaming urgency for you, it's not a problem.

We tease my brother-in-law, Randy, about a statement he made probably 25 years ago. In a moment of discussion about cholesterol, Randy proclaimed: "it's not a problem for you unless it's a problem for you." For years, we have quoted Randy on this. I can't imagine having missed that wisdom in my life. (Thanks, Randy. Give me a call when you think of something else profound.)

As I laugh, I get it. It's probably one of the more profound things I have ever heard. Its simplicity identifies a massive human tendency that I seldom factor into my daily life.

They say that the motivation behind every action is either seeking pleasure or avoiding pain. It never actually seems that simple. So, why is it that learning rarely seems to come through pleasure?

Rarely did God ever get anywhere with His people, especially his leaders, through pleasure. Brokenness and suffering seem to be His tool of choice; the broken vessel that He repairs, the dead men's bones that He revives, the suffering of the cross that brings us life, that we are healed only by His stripes.

I guess the reality is that it's not a problem for us until it is a problem for us. In pleasure or when my toe *isn't* throbbing, I simply don't see any problem. I'm certainly not motivated to change course. If it's not a problem for me, it's not a problem for me. In fact, I would go so far as to say that if it's a problem for *you* but not a problem for me, then it's not a problem.

The Experiment in Discomfort

Writing this book has created a few conflicting perspectives. I want to help others avoid being broken. I want you to learn from my pain.

The conflict is this. I know you will have your own pain, perhaps pain I may never understand. I only hope it brings us closer by understanding that our pain does not define us; it unifies us as children of God. It empowers us to emerge with renewed purpose. Instead of avoiding it, we embrace it. Instead of denying it, we own it.

We close ourselves off from relationships that cause pain. We go into denial about circumstances. In fact, we have the amazing ability to re-enact circumstances in our minds enough times that we actually believe the 'modified' version of facts.

This chapter is all about comfortable chairs. If you want to participate in a case study with me, but you don't want to actually *go* to prison, let's do this.

Remove from your life every comfortable chair you have. Take with you a plastic chair, but make sure it has no real support and sits you uncomfortably upright. No cheating. Take it with you everywhere you go. I won't even make you sleep on a top bunk, just do the plastic chair experiment. Oh, you will love this (when it's over).

Maybe you're young and agile, and it won't really matter to you. Maybe you're like me, mid-50's with a previous lower back surgery. I have an affinity for finding a comfortable chair (like the one I'm sitting in right now). This experiment becomes like a small rock in your shoe: you can deal with it at first, but over time it becomes a building agitation. Trust me, after a year of that, you swear you wouldn't complain about *anything* if you could just have a comfortable chair.

Everything is Relative

In prison, I was an off-base driver. Everyone has to have a job, and it's better than swabbing the hallways or bathroom. I think they figured I was harmless. I drove guys to the bus stations, picked up supplies, and drove the garbage to the dump. My favorite was taking guys to the doctor or hospital. There was a constant need for the 'town driver.'

There were on-base and off-base drivers. I had a good driver's license with no DUIs and a non-violent history, so I'm pretty sure I was a shoo-in. It was a great job, other than the strip searches, breathalyzers and drug tests. I got to leave the prison, to pretend I was a regular guy.

The first few times I drove back in to the prison, I felt like I was surrendering all over again. Still, it was nice to get out. I even had late night runs which were the only chance an inmate had to see the stars.

Typically, half of the trip I was alone, which was a luxury. Silence was hard to find in prison. The thing I looked forward to most was the seat in that Ford Ranger. I could never have imagined how comfortable those seats were. The plastic prison chairs made that truck seat feel like a lazy boy.

Circumstances so often dictate our perspective. After all, it's not a problem for you unless it's a problem for you. So often our circumstances drive the assessment of our condition. They define our happiness or our sense of satisfaction about life. Until that baseline is challenged or changed, it drives our model for personal fulfillment. For example, I can't be comfortable without certain chairs in my life. More accurately, unless the circumstances of my life fit my pre-defined expectations, I can't *feel* satisfied. Therefore, I cannot be happy.

None of us wants to re-write the paradigms of our lives. I got lucky enough that God himself pushed the reset button. I got a chance to experience the joy that comes completely aside from any of those paradigms. Some people find this through sickness and cancer, others through prison, others through suffering great loss. Perhaps together we can find a glimpse of true perspective through true appreciation of the comfortable chairs in our lives.

7-25-14 Journaling From Prison

It's quiet this morning, peaceful and calm. No agenda, only time. I'm sure the rush of deception still speeds on without me, a convincing timetable of someone's importance or perhaps just a march we participate in through time. Until I couldn't.

Certain of my path, I even played the drum to lead and validate the march. I imagined it to be my choice, my plan, and my honor. Still, I marched, pounding through time as milestones passed. Even the warnings emptied all my fears as my belief grew as one in the symbiotic parasitic relationship of the march...

Strangely, even departure from this pounding causes more anxiety than the inevitability found in its churning blender. Belief itself is in the routine; the belief of insanity that somewhere on that death march will be the answer of true meaning.

I have marched and would still be in step if I had not been awakened. An awakening that is more filled with reality than I ever realized. Eyes open. Living in the moment. Seeking another, narrower path.

Lord, I don't know the exact path to hear you, but I am listening. I need your presence and purpose. I am trying to let go and let you work the way you work. Empty me, Lord, and fill me with your thoughts and your Spirit. I am waiting for you. I am valued by you, according to your word. You came for me and you are my life.

7-30-14 Journaling From Prison

My Lord, thank you for your constant presence and for the joy I find in this time with you. I don't know how to express it, and I know I have only been here a week, but I feel blessed. I feel free. I feel close to you.

Finish all you have started in me, Lord, and fill me with your Holy Spirit fully, as I am open to you. I long for the fullness of your redemption. You are renewing me daily in ways I can't begin to verbalize. You are re-writing my thought processes and showing me overwhelming peace and joy when I have no reason at all circumstantially to feel peace. I am in awe. I am listening. I am yours.

Chapter Eighteen: The Visiting Room

'Humble yourselves, therefore, under God's mighty hand that he may lift you up in due time. Cast all your anxiety on him because he cares for you.' (1 Peter 5: 6-7 NIV)

It was Friday night and tomorrow Vicki would be here. I had been in prison over a week. I had made a few friends and had been invited to join their 'car.' Groups of guys working out together (I learned) called themselves a 'car.' Various cars had established their times in the gym and the other workout areas, almost like the TV room had evolved. I didn't understand it, but I had been invited so I followed along.

I had been a competitive weight lifter through high school and college. Physically, I still looked pretty formidable (albeit old and out of shape). After two shoulder surgeries, back surgery, two knee surgeries, two elbow surgeries and two wrist surgeries, I wasn't exactly in my prime. I weighed 268 pounds upon arrival. I was beginning a journey with God's blessing to inch my way toward the rejuvenation of my body. Many prayers and journal entries addressed these struggles. When I left, I had lost 45 pounds and was running 50 minutes nonstop. God literally redeemed my time.

We were halfway into a chest and triceps workout using mop handles and water jugs (no, I'm not kidding). Ed walked over to our station and raised his hand. The noise level in that small gymnasium made it hard to hear anything unless it was right next to you. I still found it impossible to understand a word that came over the PA system.

I got up from my set and walked over to Ed. "I think they just paged you to visiting," he yelled in my ear.

I replied, "No, my wife is coming tomorrow." After all, that's what we'd decided. She would drive up on as many visiting weekends as possible. She would leave early Saturday morning, stay until 3pm when visiting was over, and then drive home.

"No, I'm pretty sure they called your name," came Ed's response.

I walked up the hallway to the officers' station for verification. "Yep, Yates to visiting."

Try to picture it. I was in the middle of a workout. I hadn't shaved in three days. When I shave, I shave my entire head and face. At 55, my hair was completely white. This was *not* how I wanted to be seen by my wife after more than a week. Now my heart was pounding out of my chest. I wasn't going to let a minute be lost.

I ran to my cell and pulled my prison greens on right over the top of my sweaty workout clothes. No time to shower or shave. Friday nights were only 4:30-8:30 visiting and it was almost 5:30. I didn't want to miss a single minute. I ran up to visiting for the first time, not knowing what to expect.

I looked through the one-way glass as they patted me down. There she was. I can still feel the ache and tears that overcame me as I saw her. I felt overwhelming emotion at the thought of looking into her eyes; overwhelming pain at the thought that she was seeing me this way.

But we were together. We would be in the same room, laughing, crying, smiling into each other's spirits like nobody else on the planet could do. She was trying to be strong for me and I for her. Knowing we would be meeting exclusively like this, every other weekend, for the next 10 months or so, was difficult and beautiful.

We were together at last.

True Love

Love has never been clearer for me than it was in that visiting room. Talking for hours at a time seemed like minutes. We were thrilled doing absolutely nothing, restricted to that room with a crowd of strangers.

Very few other inmates got regular visits. Many of them lasted only an hour or two. Over years of incarceration, some had simply run out of things to say. We were lovers on a date. Starving for two weeks, we drank in each other's presence to satisfaction. Every day was a countdown to our next visit.

After a while, I began to get razzed by the other inmates. It was good natured, but perhaps also blended with jealousy. Guys would say, "come on, give her a week off for a change." They would imply that somehow I was insisting she come; trying to run her life from 'inside.' I knew I couldn't stop her even if I wanted to. What started as a logical plan to come on Saturdays every other week became Friday through Sunday, every possible visitation weekend, including every holiday.

We joked about the luxury for me to eat out of the vending machines. A burger out of vending was like prime rib. There were things in those machines you just don't get in prison, unless you're in the visiting room.

An inmate couldn't touch the money, mind you, but we could eat the food. It was always a grand gesture for visitors to make the walk up to the vending machines. When those times come, you realize just how it feels to be enslaved. I had taken freedom for granted. I had failed to understand the blessings I had been given.

The visiting room has a limit. Apparently we set it off. The officer had never seen it happen before and he didn't know what to do. I waited while the counsellor (commandant) came to check it out. Apparently there was not only the restriction to every other week, but a limit on hours each month as well.

"Why should I let you have this visit when you've already exceeded your visiting hours?" I couldn't tell if his angry face was real or not.

My answer was simple: "I'm a good guy." I smiled really big. "My wife has traveled a long way to see me." Isn't she cute? "There is nobody else in the visiting room," I reasoned.

He snarled a little, mumbled something about giving me extra duties, and waved me in. Typically, Saturday afternoons were the only busy visiting time. That room became our escape, our honeymoon, our lifeline.

Vicki stayed with her parents those Friday and Saturday nights. They lived less than two hours away. I accused Don and Elda of enjoying my prison experience because they got to see their daughter every two weeks. They also came for visits, as did my own parents and other family and friends.

Even with their own physical struggles, my mom and dad traveled over eight hours to see me at least once a month. I learned to enjoy the process of life during those times.

We shared life in that room. We shared each other. I came to love those times. It taught me how powerful it is to simply be with each other. There is no way to describe the humbling effect, watching those you love going through the invasive process of prison visitation, then experiencing their shock as you talk to them about prison life.

If you stayed for the last 20 minutes of visitation it was especially brutal. I found out the hard way that being in the 'final four' gets you strip searched. It felt as if we were being punished if we used all of the time allotted.

Inmates started bailing out half an hour early, for obvious reasons. If someone was trying to sneak contraband in, they certainly weren't going to wait to be strip searched. It wasn't about finding anything, it was about the exertion of power over us. Humiliating us. Breaking us.

Saying goodbye was terrible. Waving goodbye as they walk away, crying as you watched their tears, overwhelmed with extreme joy and sorrow, then following a C.O. (corrections officer) to a restroom or shower stall to be strip searched... it was just terrible.

Then I collapsed. The expanse of emotion spent was too much. I watched Vicki drive away. She had a four-and-a-half hour drive alone, and was as emotionally exhausted as I was. I prayed for her safety, that her tears wouldn't interfere. She was going home to an empty house and I couldn't do anything to comfort her. These are emotions I will never forget.

I caused them all. I tried to live in my own strength. I worshipped my own idol. I believed in myself as my own god. In the visiting room, I found out that there were still areas of my heart to be broken.

Connected Through Shared Pain

We have many funny stories from the visiting room. We met the families of other inmates and felt like friends. We shared a common situation and common pain.

Sharing pain is possibly the greatest bonding agent. It renders your past, history, race or part of the country irrelevant. We shared a foxhole and we could relate to each other. I found myself caring for them and their families. Vicki even felt compelled to send money to a family in need.

We realized how blessed we were, even in the visiting room. We didn't have much, but we had each other and we had our family. We had the Lord.

Vicki told me something special before I left for prison. I remember it vividly: "Greg, everything we need, we have." At another time, she blurted out something not quite so eloquent: "Well, it could be worse. You could be dead."

She was right. God had given me a chance to live through the storm; through the bloody battle, and I wasn't dead.

During my incarceration, I lost three friends unexpectedly to aggressive cancers. God was breaking me, but I wasn't dead. In fact, it might be the ultimate opportunity of my life. To be salt and light, even when I felt trampled into the ground, it was a chance to give strength to others when I had no strength of my own. The will to praise God when no circumstances seemed to call for it; learning to give thanks in *all* circumstances.

I am thankful to be alive *and* to be broken.

Visiting Room Wisdom

The blood and water of my brokenness flowed together. Through the Spirit of the Lord, I began to see parallels I'd never even imagined. I learned what it was like to spend hours talking with God, having no agenda, just like the visiting room. I learned to be humbled in front of Him and realized that He loved me anyway. He came any length required to be with me in my greatest need. He had already sacrificed to create a lifeline to me. He made preparations for this day long before I knew it was coming.

He brought me close to people I would never have known. He allowed me to see the horror of life without Him and the power the enemy has over so many. He showed me that 'everything I need, I have' in Him.

He reminded me I wasn't dead. He showed me I was never more alive than when I exchanged the cares of life for freedom that only He could give; a freedom that only came when I was completely and utterly broken.

I look forward to my time with the Lord every day, just like the visiting room. I come without an agenda. I don't have anything in my hands or my pockets. I feed on the food He brings me, purchased by His own blood. I can't buy anything of my own. I have nothing of value anyway. I am completely dependent on Him.

I love my personal freedom. I never want to return to the life of baggage and busyness. I was created to spend time with my creator and to receive from the blessings He planned from the beginning.

Lord, let me be your vessel. Let me follow your precepts, fully dependent on your strength.

I am released into your custody and set free into your care.

When I grew up, I heard people talk about their prayer closet. For me, it will always be the visiting room.

7-28-14 Journaling From Prison

Oh, my Father. God of all creation. Keeper of the secrets of your plan and your fullness. Radiant giver of Glory through your presence, increased by our openness to your flow of life and energy, as you long to share yourself with us. With me.

I believe in you, in your careful plan and generous grace. I have proven to be no different from other men who have failed to perceive the Truth and have followed my own way. But your persistence has burst forth in a volume of perception that is just too much for words. I have seen your love, but also your jealous passion.

I don't know how to do this… but you do. You are the relentless force that cannot be resisted. You are water, finding its way through the cracks and seeping into the voids of my soul. You are fullness and vacuum at the same time, which is beyond explanation and beyond the will of man.

The enemy resists, but cannot prevail. By your stripes I am healed. I am broken and useless on my own. You make the hardened clay useful again. You redeem and restore, even my life. I long to redeem myself, but such arrogance and idolatry has no more place in my weakness. Thank you for my weakness. Let it be so, according to your will and your power and purpose. Amen.

Chapter Nineteen: Don't Be Afraid

'But the Advocate, the Holy Spirit, whom the Father will send in my name, will teach you all things and will remind you of everything I have said to you. Peace I leave with you; my peace I give you. I do not give to you as the world gives. Do not let your hearts be troubled <u>and do not be afraid</u>.' (John 14: 25-27 NIV)

It was a beautiful day. Not only that, but I was scheduled to take Ramon to the doctor's office. I would be on the road or sitting in the doctor's office from around 8am until mid-afternoon. What a lucky break. When every day looked the same, these opportunities were rare and priceless.

I microwaved a full cup of instant coffee, stuffed some almonds and a book in my oversized coat pocket, and headed for the C.O.'s office to sign out for the trip. The trip procedure was very detailed. It included a ride down to transportation to pick up a vehicle and a phone. There were three numbers programmed into the phone for emergencies, and it tracked our movements.

After signing out, we headed for the car. For the next several hours we would pretend we were normal. We were just normal guys driving to the doctor together wearing green uniforms, carrying institutional clear coffee cups. It all seemed normal until, inevitably, we intersected with the outside world.

The smallest convenience has tremendous value when you are in prison. A paperclip, a rubber band, a letter from someone—anyone. It took weeks for me to tolerate the instant coffee on commissary, but soon I couldn't imagine anything better. After living in the companionship of 200 guys wearing green uniforms, you soon fit right in. Your comparisons make you feel pretty good about the weight you've lost, the way you look, and the normalcy of things.

When you're in prison, one size fits all. Everyone has the same clear plastic thermal coffee mug and water bottle, and eats the same meals. Topics of conversation and gossip revolve around 'inmate.com' (we don't have internet access, this is sarcastic reference to unreliable information). The items of interest involved the menu, the weather, the officer's schedules and institution movies showing that weekend. There were endless conversations about people's 'cases.' Time stands still in prison. The last thing inmates remember about their 'other' life is often their interaction with prosecutors, lawyers and judges.

I started the trip with a full cup of hot coffee, and by the time we arrived, it was cold. The thermal cups from prison were intentionally clear so nobody could hide anything in them. When it is completely stained with coffee, it's pretty gross. You don't remember how ridiculous they look until you enter the 'real world.'

I walked into the doctor's office with Ramon. While I was waiting, one of the receptionists caught my eye. "Do you need anything while you're waiting? We have vending machines." The awkwardness of the statement was even more exaggerated because she was a woman. The only women we saw, with exception of the visiting room, were wearing uniforms. They weren't typically concerned or friendly.

"I appreciate that, but I don't have any money," I replied. "Do you have a microwave where I could warm up my coffee?"

She smiled and walked toward me, holding out her hand for my cup. "Sure."

The look on her face was priceless. I'm sure mine was as well. I handed her my clear, coffee-stained cup and knew she was wondering if it would be rude to retreat for a pair of latex gloves. With just two fingers carefully holding it, she disappeared behind the reception desk. A couple minutes later, she returned with a paper towel wrapped around my cup. I thanked her and resisted the urge to laugh, cry or shrink into the woodwork.

Accepting the reality of my new persona was difficult. I was nobody special. I was labeled, debased, and unfit for even casual interaction with society. I drove through towns slowly and looked at people engaged in their everyday activities. I was a foreigner. I had exchanged my S550 Mercedes for a Ford Ranger. People looked at me with fear or contempt, or tried not to look at all.

On another occasion, I took Nick (these names have been changed, by the way), a very large, tattooed Puerto Rican inmate, to have surgery on his shoulder. Nick had been 'down' for a long time. He looked rough, but he was a pretty good guy. He looked intimidating as we walked into the hospital.

I proceeded to make myself comfortable with the coffee, almonds and commissary snacks I had brought. Within minutes, I saw an older lady from admissions wringing her hands as she scanned the lobby. She made brief eye contact with me, then looked away. Finally I walked over to inquire.

"Uh," she stammered, "are you here with Nick?"

"Yes, I am," I replied.

"Um… where is the officer?"

"Well ma'am, Nick has approval to come without an officer and I am here as his escort."

"Oh. Generally, there is an officer," she seemed to struggle to say.

I smiled. "Ma'am, if there is any issue, please let me help."

Still a little shaky, she looked me in the eye. "Ok."

I assured her we were some of the good guys. I wondered how it felt to be in her shoes. Later, as Nick's surgery progressed, I was apparently considered Nick's family. They gave me updates, offered me snacks and called me in when he went to recovery. I'm not sure the HIPPA laws were completely adhered to, but the prison wasn't very concerned about obeying the letter of the law anyway.

After loading up a few snacks which couldn't be purchased in our commissary (I even made some toast), I was led to Nick's room. They asked me to help him get his clothes on. I asked, "Nick, do you need help getting dressed?"

"Naw," he replied.

"Good," I growled. I left, laughing my way back to the waiting area. We may have been brothers in one sense, but I wasn't ready to nurse him back to health.

When the nurse talked to me at his release, she said, "Now, he will need to have a comfortable place to lay down." *Uh, not likely, ma'am. He will have the same as everyone else.* "Don't let his pain medicine get behind. He has a nerve block now, but in about 14 hours it is going to come alive. The pain will be hard to get under control if he doesn't already have pain meds in his system." *Yes, ma'am, but that is out of my control.*

I passed off all this information and Nick's records to the infirmary at the prison. It was two days before Nick received any meds.

Before we left the hospital, we had an amazing opportunity. "If you want to wait another fifteen minutes, we can bring you dinner from the hospital cafeteria."

Wow. Food. Food that wasn't prison food. Even hospital food had to be better, right?

I could do an entirely separate chapter about 'food porn,' as we called it in prison: guys cutting out pictures of food and plastering them on the walls. I drove the box truck to pick up food for the prison sometimes. The frozen cases ranged from 3-5 years past expiration. We ate a lot of rice and beans.

I stepped into Nick's recovery room and his bleary eyes met mine. "Nick, they say we can get dinner here in a few minutes."

I mistakenly thought he would be as excited as I was. "Naw, man. We got to *go*. It's Thursday, chicken day. We got to go. I got to get my fried chicken."

Despite explaining that I had already requested they save us trays and we could eat *both* meals, he was beside himself. "WE GOT TO GO."

In that moment, I learned the meaning of the word 'institutionalized.'

Released, but Seldom Free

As impossible as it seems, we rarely resist our bondage. We resist change. When our experiences become normal for us, we don't need to be tied down any longer.

Our coffee mugs seem perfectly normal. The coffee tastes fine, even if we are tapping the water straight out of a hot water heater (not kidding). Our attire is just fine. We stand by the bed to be counted at 10pm whether we are being counted or not. Such is the truth with any form of incarceration, whether imposed on us or imposed by us.

I took more than 100 men from the medium security prison to bus and train stations. They were heading home or to a half-way house. For most, the fear outweighed the excitement. Statistically, over 85% of them would return to prison. I wondered what the statistics were for people trying to break free from their own prisons of compartmentalized reality and self-imposed identity.

Being released is only the beginning of a long process of reintegration. At times, sensory inputs were overwhelming for a man who's been incarcerated. Many men, once we arrived at our final destination, asked permission to get out of the truck. The smell of perfume or the sights and sounds of freedom can be like triggering PTSD.

Even greater than the challenges are the expectations. Our own, and the expectations of others… sometimes it's just easier to fail. To prove them right.

As a driver, I asked lots of questions of my inmate passengers. I transported inmates who had been incarcerated as many as 30 years. I heard their stories and their fears. Could they find a job? Could they take care of their children? Would they be able to stay off drugs?

On one of the trips, I asked someone if he believed in God. He said yes. I asked if he felt God could make a real difference in his life, for his future and with respect to his fears. He paused, then softly said yes.

As we pulled into the bus station, I felt the overwhelming presence of the Holy Spirit. Before he got out of the car, I asked if I could pray for him. He melted. I knew God had a plan. "Can I put my hand on your shoulder?" He nodded. I knew enough not to touch him without permission.

My attempt to pray was awkwardly and innately human. He thanked me and got out. As I turned the truck back toward prison, I was overwhelmed with the Spirit of the Lord. I prayed and cried aloud the entire trip. I prayed for this man and his family, and that God would prepare someone else to engage him in the faith. The overwhelming realization was that God could use me, even as an inmate. God did use me.

That moment changed me. My mind flashed back to that late night prayer with a troubled employee. I felt I was the hand of Jesus, reaching out. I felt the satisfaction of my Father. Nothing I had tried to achieve previously even came close.

The tears come as I re-live that moment. My life was not about me. I cared more about someone else than myself. I was glad to be there. I was thrilled to be grafted into the vine of Jesus Christ. He was flowing through me, bearing fruit as only He can.

My Secret Mission

It felt like a covert operation. I wasn't sure if my mobile chapel would get me into trouble or not. I didn't advertise it. I asked a few Christian inmates to pray for me. I tried to be sensitive to this mission. I found myself praying every trip for the next six months that God would give me the courage and the right words. They weren't always receptive. I prayed with a lot more than I didn't. It felt like food from Heaven.

I can still see the eyes, even the tears many of these men cried. Some even prayed with me. Some grabbed my hand to pursue God together. It was rare for an inmate to touch anyone else. Most of these men I would never have known outside prison: gang members, drug dealers, guys with long histories of violence. I'm not the prettiest tool in the shed, so they probably thought the same of me. My life was changed forever as I comprehended Jesus himself, reaching across to touch their lives.

More than once, after arriving back to the prison, I was asked why my eyes were so red. It cost me additional drug tests, in fact. The saturation of the Holy Spirit was far more addicting than anything I could have ingested. I never want to forget.

The Prison I Built For Myself

Driving back to the prison one day, I had a thought, like a voice speaking to me: *don't be afraid.*

I was startled. "I'm not afraid," I said aloud. I couldn't think of anything I was afraid of. I was not afraid, but it came again: don't be afraid. I turned on the Christian radio station for a change of pace. At that precise moment, the host was reading 1 John 4:18:

'Where God's love is, there is no fear, because God's perfect love drives out fear. It is punishment that makes a person fear, so love is not made perfect in the person who fears.'

I knew the Lord was speaking to me, but I didn't know what I was supposedly afraid of. I didn't want to be labeled crazy, so I kept it to myself. Over the next day, however, the thought of bottling fear inside myself would not leave me.

I decided to make a list. During noon census the next day, I sat with a notebook to list any possible fears, anything God might be talking to me about. I was generally thinking about my family, ongoing legal issues, finances and the like. As the pen hit the paper, only one word came to mind: insignificance.

I have never felt insignificant. Suddenly, the concept floated through my consciousness, as if set free by my spoken acknowledgment. It clamored like a pinball machine, racking up points. A cascade of uncontrolled realizations ensued.

Compartments which had been camouflaged were sprung open. God was probing the deepest sand-covered premise of my existence. Touching the very point of my need.

146

I was institutionalized by the prison of my own making. I was a prisoner who carried grubby coffee cups like the whitewashed tombs of my life. I was an inmate who was insistent on 'chicken day' rather than the fulfillment of God's divine plan.

In my house there were many rooms to shield me from the way, the truth and the *life,* if it didn't meet my criteria. These compartments kept me from experiencing the environment outside my prison… even a Holy environment.

I kept working to define my own significance, no matter how distorted or obscene. I would never have ceased the effort of fabricating significance. Finally, apart from my own strength, wisdom or actions, I was set free. I was broken.

Don't be afraid.

7-29-14 Journaling From Prison

Set me free, Lord, with you. All my thoughts and perspectives. All my capacities and all my plans. Set me free from myself and the limits I have placed on you. You are King and commander of all things. You have caused all of this to bring me back to you. To show me your plan. I am so lucky to be the object of your affection, to feel the influence of the Spirit in my thoughts and know that I am moving closer. Not by my own strength, because that would be laughable, but by your compassion and care.

You are forcing me to be honest with myself, to let go of pride and self-accomplishment. Let me fully release and admit the influence of sin that was in my life, consuming me from the inside out. I release that to you, Lord. I know you have forgiven me. Help me to fully forgive myself. I take responsibility for my decisions and I cling to your grace. I have so many regrets, yet you used all of that and brought me to yourself. Thank you.

Chapter Twenty: Right Where He Wants Me

'You, God, know my folly; my guilt is not hidden from you. Lord, the Lord Almighty, may those who hope in you not be disgraced because of me… But I pray to you, Lord, in the time of your favor; in your great love, O God, answer me with your sure salvation. Rescue me from the mire, do not let me sink; deliver me from those who hate me, from the deep waters.' (Psalm 69: 5-6a, 13-14 NIV)

The room was beyond capacity as I walked to the front with my notes in hand. I'd spoken to many groups before, but speaking in prison wasn't anything like that. It felt like I had just finished baseball season with the most strikeouts in the league and they wanted me to tell everyone how I managed it.

Life is full of twists that seem illogical. Somehow, we just roll on through them. There is an old saying that applies: in the land of the blind, the one-eyed man is king. I guess I was the one-eyed man tonight.

So, let's talk about business. It was a discussion with around 100 inmates about starting your own business. I asked Tim, one of my cellies, to write on the whiteboard as everyone gave their reasons to be in business. The list was long: "I want to be my own boss," "I want to make more money," "I want more free time," "I want …"

We are all idealistic, optimistic dreamers. Business fantasies are the worst. That night, I shared a lot about the demands of business, but like the strike-out king I spent most of my time talking about how I got it wrong. All I could see was the failure.

I flashed back to a job we had in the early 90's to build an injection mold for a scrub brush. It was an innovative design. We quoted the tool so expensive we didn't think there was a chance of getting the job. Nesting segmented cores that had to release and retract every shot. Exotic runner systems to fill them and exquisite venting to exhaust the air from each cavity. It was all the excitement a young design team could ask for.

Don't we all love theory? (Which reminds me... Have you ever seen a business plan that didn't make money? I haven't.) Before the scrub brush job was over, I had visions of going back in time to write the customer a $10,000 check to beg them not to give us the job.

Education is expensive. Ego and pride are *expensive*. We take on every giant in life, believing we can conquer it. What if we aren't always intended to win?

What if you could trust that there is a purpose for all of the things that seem pointless? What if you were supposed to travel the path exactly the way you were traveling it?

How did you meet your wife, your best friend? How did you get your job or end up living where you live? If you're like me, you know that more than one of the enormous parts of your life seemed to happen accidentally. If you hadn't been at a certain place at a certain time, having a random conversation with a random person, your life would be very different. You are still walking that path to the ultimate destination.

There is always more going on than we realize.

Don't Bother Me With the Facts

15 is a scary age. Girls, driver's education, pimples. I remember it well. One day I stumbled across a 1969 Camaro I absolutely had to have. When I looked at that car, all that registered was wide tires, loud music and attracting girls.

I begged my dad to look at the car with me. I needed his help and permission to buy it. What he saw in that car was strangely different. He saw leaking oil, a motor that was rough and exhaust that was shot, tires that were nearly bald and a hood that had been up and down more times than a cookie jar. It was a disaster.

But I wanted it. He was trying to destroy my dreams. He didn't want me to have anything I wanted.

Sometimes I'm guilty of making decisions about life and business that way, aren't you? We see the pitfalls. Of course, if *we* were in the driver's seat, we could do it better than anyone else. *We* can make it work. Capital? Cash flow? The last five guys who failed? Doesn't matter… we have our dream.

Have you ever tried to talk someone out of a decision with disaster written all over it? Could you literally see the trance they were in? I have news for you: at some point, we all experience it. *I'm different and that will never happen to me.* It's a powerful illusion.

Is life really all about a gut feeling, having a hunch and following it? Do we take a shot on a 'lucky number' or ride the momentum of a lucky streak? Sometimes my life felt like a rollercoaster full of thrills, but which took me nowhere.

I never realized it was possible to know that I was right where I was supposed to be.

The Birth of New Momentum

Coming face-to-face with biblical business principles was almost insulting. I was worth more than 30 million dollars and had successful businesses clicking along every day. I was serving on multiple boards of directors and had a large team of managers accountable to me.

One day, an older gentleman came into my office. By reputation, I knew Albert. He always provided a guarded curiosity to me. He had the ear of many successful people in the area and I figured they couldn't all be wrong.

He didn't wear his past successes or influence loudly. He was easy spoken and gave you the feeling that he had arrived before you saw him. He was one of those guys you just 'felt.' Strangely, he reminded me of my own father.

We sat for a moment. I struggled to dig out some sweetener for his coffee. My motto had always been "you can tell the strength of a business by the strength of its coffee." Clearly Albert had toned down by this point. His thick Dutch accent forced me to focus.

I felt a calm that melted my rigid clock-watching. He shared with me and I shared with him. Knowing he was a Christian, I felt obligated to extol the Christian theme of my life. I shared my past, all God's blessings in my life. Albert failed to respond with the awe I had come to expect. He kept asking me questions that were irritating, about my thoughts on various principles of business in the bible. It was as if he already knew I was in violation of them.

Theory and principles are great, but I live in the real world. You are either all-in or not.

Albert offered to teach a class about God's principles for business. Apparently, according to Albert, there were more than 2000 scriptures related to business in the bible. The only topic covered more was love. "Sounds great... Yeah, let's do that sometime. Have your people call my people."

Eventually, I offered him an office in our building. He needed a place to 'land' once in a while. He was retired and sometimes it's just nice to get out of the house. Little did I know that his 'mentoring' would ooze its way around the building to some 45 people working in our corporate offices. It was a little annoying at times. I always maintained (what I called) a 60 second rule. Go ahead and talk about last night or the kids, but keep it to about 60 seconds. We are here to produce.

I remember the day I accidentally got copied into an organization-wide email. My assistant was trying to coordinate the purchase of coffee for the break room. Everyone's contributions, the procedures, her plan to collect on a certain day... apparently they had been doing this for some time.

After seeing a dozen or more 'reply-all' responses, I responded: *I don't want to see any more responses to this email. We are wasting time on this. I will resolve the coffee issue. Karen, please come to my office RIGHT NOW.*

In adherence to my 'strong coffee' mantra, I put in a professional coffee maker. Everybody's coffee was *free.* Drink all you want. It was the most positive employee benefit I offered in several years. More importantly, it assuaged my overwhelming anxiety about people wasting time.

Now I had Albert having personal conversations with people, talking to them about their motives, counseling them. Didn't he know that he was costing me money?

I had no idea at the time that God placed Albert in my life. God planted seed in my heart through Albert that I would not be ready to hear for several years. God used Albert to begin a process I didn't even realized was taking place. God was already saving me.

One day, in the midst of a crisis, Albert popped into my office and wondered if I had time. Not wanting to be rude, I offered him a coffee and we sat down. I was under pressure and not fully engaged with him. "Greg... God's got you right where he wants you."

What? I sighed deeply. Ok, I guess I can see that. He has put me in this position of responsibility. He has given me these gifts and He has done it so I can resolve this crisis. He is cheering me on because I am right where he wants me. (Right?)

That was my logic, anyway. Little did I know I was not the 'man of the hour.' The true tenor of the message was still unseen. He had me where *He* wanted me, for *His* purpose. This was for my redemption, for my restoration as his son, but first the vessel had to be broken.

What's My Purpose?

Until recently, I prayed this prayer every day:

Lord, show me what you want me to do.

Show me the career you want me to pursue.

Show me your will and I WILL DO IT.

(I am so consistent... Do, Do, Do.)

I prayed as if God would open up my eyes. Then I would charge off into the sunset. I wanted God to provide, but I wanted Him to provide through me.

Don't you admire people who are absolute in their objective? Sometimes I felt cheated.

I have some news. I consider it good news. *God has you right where He wants you.*

Let me build this from the bottom up. I was conflicted whenever I tried to answer these 'mystical questions' about life's purpose. I loved it when a sci-fi TV show pulled out an 'oracle' or an 'orb' that would give people answers beyond their own wisdom.

At times, I felt I had a clear vision. I could see what God was doing and what He wanted from me. With my adrenaline pumping, I puked passion on everyone. It was accompanied by a fierceness that kept anyone from disagreeing with me.

I admired that guy. He was powerful and strong and focused. He was intimidating. He was also a failure who ultimately ended up in prison.

Albert returned to my office after I had been indicted for bank fraud. I couldn't even lift my eyes to his. He said the one thing he knew was the only absolute truth: "Greg… God has you right where He wants you."

For the first time, I began to capture the image of 'not one stone being left upon another.' The cornerstone was finally being put in place. Could God really use the brokenness of my life? Could I truly depend on His word and His principles when I had blown up everything I ever built?

I was determined to find out.

1-26-15 Journaling in Prison

As I pilfer through this compost heap, I feel like I can see and feel the synapses still firing, like a robot with circuits spread all over the floor; disconnected. Some still make me flinch, but their continuity no longer stays intact. The perfectly constructed machine has been disrupted by your call, Lord, and the deep, quiet cry of my heart for a savior.

I could barely hear it myself, but its whimper surfaced as each compartment cycled in the few remaining quiet moments. A cry only you could hear. A groan you could not ignore. A cry that brought you powerfully to my rescue, disarming every bond that held my facade in place. Shattering the building materials of straw and sticks, quaking the sand of my foundation. Reaching out your hand to me. In my despair, you heard my cry and delivered me. Out of my bondage, you saved me.

Strange, how painful the straps of bondage were when removed. I prayed you would not rip them from my flesh, the flesh of my heart, for they bled and hurt so badly; but you knew. You knew the flesh of my heart could not grow over the barbed wire of my bondage and become a perfect heart as you created me to be. Even now, a few thorns surface that must be removed.

Hold me, Lord. Heal me. Love me.

Chapter Twenty-One: Finally Home

'I am the vine; you are the branches. If you remain in me and I in you, you will bear much fruit; apart from me you can do nothing.' (John 15: 5 NIV)

For almost 10 months, everything had been a countdown. I counted days to each visit. When Vicki and I talked on the phone, we always ended with "11 days and a wake up." I inherited that lingo from the boys. As I scratched my way toward my release date, I began to count other things as well. I will need seven more razor blades, two more jars of peanut butter, and three more laundry cards. It was the countdown.

Months felt like years. Days felt like weeks. Once you are a 'short-timer,' everyone starts the countdown. Every conversation starts with "How many days?" I'm pretty sure the counting made it worse. Other inmates loved the countdowns. The day I arrived, I remember Tim telling me he couldn't wait until I was gone, "'cause I'll be that much closer to the door."

It's fun to start giving stuff away. You buy the things you need, but you don't have any desire to take them with you. The smallest convenience items are treasured 'inside.'

I started to dream about being home. The touch of the people you love. The quiet. Sleeping in your own bed. Taking a shower without shower shoes. The food. The coffee (had to sneak that in there). We started making plans for the first meals and the family getting together. I hadn't seen most of them for almost a year.

Vicki would make one last trip. This time, I would walk out the door with her. I couldn't drive yet, even though I had been driving the entire time I was "down." My prison issued driver's license wasn't good enough anymore.

I began training a replacement driver a month before my out-date. Soon he was getting some of my trips, and that made the weeks even longer. Finally, three days before my release, I was posted as inactive; I was done driving. Time came to a grinding halt.

Finally, it was my last night in prison. Just before 10pm count, I was paged to the office. I hadn't seen this officer before. He asked me if I was aware I had a trip that night. Night trips were always to Tomah, Wisconsin and it was a good two and a half hours round-trip. Generally we left around midnight, which meant most of the night's sleep was lost. I wouldn't be able to sleep anyway.

When I returned to the facility, the strangest thing happened: a guard met me in a panic. I had a lot more experience than he did with process and procedure, as it turns out.

"Get out of here," he commanded. "Come back in 20 minutes. You'll mess up my paperwork."

During the night, there were three 'flashlight' counts where the officers walked the halls and counted by shining a flashlight on each inmate. Two guards made the count so they could compare numbers. You had to be certain some part of your body was sticking out from under the covers. Once they get a count, they call it in and prepare paperwork to be picked up by the perimeter driver.

When you leave for a trip, you sign a furlough. You are no longer included in the prison population. Once, when I was gone on the library run, they had the place locked down because their count was off. Turns out they were looking for me because I was not properly taken off the system. Now I had returned and he had one more prisoner than his paperwork should have. He wanted me gone until the paperwork cleared.

I had to laugh. "No problem," I replied, and headed out the door for a drive through the country.

When I returned, he was waiting at the door with cigarettes in hand. "Go on in and I'll sign you in after my break." This would also be the first and only time I re-entered the facility without a breathalyzer. I shook my head and did as I was told. It was a night to remember. I was leaving in about four hours and soaking up every experience for the last time.

People streamed by my cell to say goodbye. We exchanged contact information, even though we knew it probably wouldn't happen. It was a show of friendship. A nod that our connection was real. I cared about these guys, but today I was ready for so much more. Today I would be free. Today I could hold Vicki's hand. We could buy real food. I could fire up my old cell phone and let my anxious family know I was out.

Even though it was only ten months, I felt different. I felt the restraints even though they weren't there. I felt the lingering brain damage. I wasn't really going back, I was going forward. I knew this would be a completely new life.

I placed my cardboard box of papers, books and journals into the back seat. Vicki had clothes for me to change into. She brought the smallest jeans I had in the closet, but they were sagging off of me. It felt so good to have jeans on again.

There were a lot of hurdles ahead. A lot of restrictions, a lot of limitations, but I would be home. Nothing else mattered.

Abundance I Don't Deserve

I'm sitting on the back deck of our home. God chose to preserve this spot for me to return to. I think He did it just to show me how much He loves me. I met with the Lord many times here in the two years prior to my incarceration. I think He wanted to show me the continuity of His presence.

I'm looking out over flowers (I have no idea what most of them are). They were planted by Vicki, who knows every flower, every plant, every bird song, and every grandchild's story. She invested wisely over the past 35 years while I was busy making other plans. I see the intricate beauty I had nothing to do with. I have no power over it.

While writing in my journal this morning, I decided I would take a walk around the yard. I thanked God openly for the day and all of this beauty. Yes, it's summer. I might not be as thankful when I'm shoveling snow.

I snipped off some onions and lettuce in the garden. Blossoms from zucchini and cucumbers were everywhere. I thanked God for His amazing provision.

I pondered how far we have come in the name of progress. We were given everything and yet we substitute it all in the pursuit of man-made forms of currency. It seems we prefer to buy man-made creations. I was leading the pack. In my quest, an endless progression of Mercedes, sports cars and airplanes completely ignored the most satisfying things in life.

I looked toward the blackberry trellises. Spread out and beautiful, I checked a few bulging berries to see if they would fall off in my hand. Vicki is very specific about the procedure for picking blackberries. I love procedure. I gently tugged and they held fast. There are going to be a lot of berries ready in the next few days.

159

Suddenly, the sunlight at the top of the trellis caught my attention. It played on a vine that had wound four or five loops around the wooden standard. The leaves looked similar to the berries, but the vine was much smaller in diameter and a lighter color. Ah… a parasite. It was trying to choke out my vines. It worked its way through their strength to steal their nutrients and sunlight.

I went to work. I didn't want to simply break it off, I wanted to find the root and remove it. As I worked, unwound and untangled, I began to realize this was not just one vine. There were dozens of rapidly growing vines working their way through the entire area. I admired their method as I struggled to trace them through the fruitful berry vines. I didn't want to damage anything.

Their tenacity and their intricacy was brilliant. The good vine completely supported them. They were very well camouflaged. The scripture came to me about the wheat and the tares. Ultimately, even if not before the harvest, they will be separated and the tares will be thrown into the fire.

I felt a tremor as I traced the parasitic vines. It wasn't just the poison ivy popping up nearby; I knew the Spirit of God was talking to me about *me*. I had allowed so many parasitic vines to grow up in my life that I couldn't even recognize them. Ultimately, the entire vineyard had to be cut down in order to separate the good from the bad.

If I could have prayed my way out of a full pruning, I would have. My Father, the gardener, knows how to care for His creation. It was a long time before I was ready to hear the truth that He can be trusted, that He knows what he is doing, and that everything He was doing to me was for my salvation.

It was my Father, disciplining the son He loves, grafting me back into the vine to produce good fruit.

I'm Tired of Trying to Bear Fruit

I can't help noticing the Hostas. In the spring, they struggled to poke little green shoots out of the ground. It seemed that overnight they burst upward impossibly. Today, they are enormous leaves on four foot plants. I am reminded of the scripture: *can any of you, by worrying, add one single inch to your height?* We are like those Hostas. They were designed and empowered to fulfill a purpose of beauty and nuance. God purposed it all and it happens. It just happens.

I spent a lifetime trying to *will* myself into a flowering state; to achieve my way toward the sky and force fruit onto my limbs. The man-made adhesive holding it to my branches has failed. It lies on the ground and I strain even harder. I live in the anxiety of decisions. I beg God to help me fulfill my purpose and achieve goals I have set.

The concept of the vine and the branches is completely inverted; the expectations I have for myself are completely upside down. I live under the assumption that I must find a way to please God. I strive to overcome my obstacles. I battle to provide security for my family and fulfillment for my life. I strain to squeeze into the next 10 years what I have failed to fulfill in the last 30.

I get the logic of how fruit has to be borne, but I want to create fruit in my own way (or so it seems). Can I really provide *no inertia* to bearing that fruit? Is my mission relegated to remaining in the vine, preventing any obstruction from obscuring the path of its life-giving nutrients? Is that really my entire mission?

Am I just a puppet? Can't I create? Did God design me to be truly one with Him, or to simply play with the toys I can understand in a physical universe?

Oneness with the Father comes only by faith (for now), and will someday be by sight. Seeing how God works simply isn't possible for us yet, but knowing that He works is. We are preparing ourselves for an eternity in which we will experience that oneness on a level beyond our imagination.

I am no longer satisfied to live as I have lived in the past. I want to live as God intended me to live, bearing His fruit in my life both now and forever.

That is the fruit I was intended to bear.

Chapter Twenty-Two: While I Was Making Other Plans

'And we boast in the hope of the Glory of God. Not only so, but we also glory in our sufferings, because we know that suffering produces perseverance; perseverance, character; and character, hope. And hope does not put us to shame, because God's love has been poured out into our hearts through the Holy Spirit, who has been given to us.'
(Romans 5: 2b-5 NIV)

It had to happen sooner or later.

We were standing in the foyer of the church. Our friends, John and Sara, were introducing us to one of their pastors. I had been home only a couple of months. This was the first trip my parole officer had approved outside the district. Stepping out into the real world felt great. I could breathe again.

Suddenly, out of nowhere, it happened. I suppose I should have been prepared for it. All he did was ask the age old question we use to define ourselves. We perfect the answering of this question because it quietly postures our ego and our status. It is who we purport to be, perhaps even who we believe we are; it is our identity.

"So Greg, what do you do?" There it was. The question flushed my head with an instant blast of adrenaline and I began frantically searching for an appropriate response.

I did consider answering truthfully just to see his reaction. *Well, I just got out of prison so I'm pretty much living off of my wife these days.* Before I could answer in any capacity, John jumped in to divert the topic.

As strange as it sounds, I haven't had the urge to introduce myself as a felon, an ex-con, a criminal. Tell me, how am I supposed to identify with others in this new sector of life? I want to get it right. If I'm not careful, I will build on the old foundation once again. My elevator speech will begin the construction of new walls to maintain. It may be the greatest temptation I have faced; so many natural desires to be fulfilled, disclaimers I want to give, footholds that want to lock themselves back into place.

How do I make a break between the old way of thinking and the new? The curse of idolatry and pride find new ways to assert themselves. I struggle to know who I am, now that I have been newly uncovered by the grace of God. As I try to define it, the only things that come out seem negative:

- I don't trust myself.
- I don't know what lies ahead of me and I can't plan for it.
- I can't see ten steps or ten days ahead of myself.
- I have no idea what tomorrow is going to be like or the plans I should make.

I don't know who I am anymore. All I know is that my beliefs are changing me at my very core. Very soon, I must have beliefs that are actionable. I want to look beyond what I can see, to

164

see beyond what I can calculate. I want to have the audacity to believe that God has me right where He wants me and that He has been bringing me to this point my entire life. I want to believe that He has a plan to prosper me and not to harm me. I want to trust Him. I really do.

Urgency vs. Faith

God picked me up from the bottom. Immediately, my first prayers trended back to where I had lived before. God, what do you want me to *do?*

Surely there is a plan, a career, a bunch of instructions for me to *do.*

'But seek first His kingdom and His righteousness, and all these things will be given to you as well.' (Matthew 6: 33 NIV)

Of course I know that scripture, but I have spent a year trying to figure out what it means… in me.

God, don't you know I have deadlines? I have decisions to make and bills to pay. Yes I want your will, but I need it *now.*

God has never had the kind of urgency that I have. He frustrates me because I am a planner. He is before me, behind me, beside me and beyond my comprehension, but He doesn't seem to own a watch or a calendar. He asks me to trust Him but He doesn't explain anything He's doing. How am I supposed to know what He wants me to *do?*

Maybe you're like me in this regard. I want to believe, but I want a belief that is actionable. I want to learn and then plan and then take action. Does that sound right to you? After all, everything in life is moving forward and we can't just wait for something to come to us, right?

Seeing Beyond the Situation

Sitting in the deposition made everything more real. I had been so busy trying to battle for my own survival that it hadn't occurred to me how we would survive financially.

"So Mr. Yates, tell me about any jewelry you or your wife own. Does she have a wedding ring?" The bank's attorney was nonchalant as he probed through our life and presented document after document identifying everything I owned. We had provided the documentation as ordered, and now it was being used to search for anything that could be sold or surrendered. My retirement account was already being called into question because Vicki had not contributed to it, only me. Soon everything that could be liquidated was on a list and I was expected to comply.

As he looked through our corporate brochure, he walked from company to company asking for more information. In the brochure, our franchise sub shops were listed but I had not provided any information about their ownership.

"Why don't we have any information about this company?" he asked.

Without hesitation, my own attorney informed him that I had no ownership in that company. It was owned by my wife, who was the day-to-day operator as well. After ownership documentation was produced, we moved on.

That was one of the few things I accidentally did right. At that moment, I grinned. Every time I think about this, I am keenly aware that God was planting seed in our lives long before we knew we needed it.

Back in 2003, we had a lot of cash available and were looking for investments. An employee knew of a franchise sub shop whose owners were ready to sell and move out of the area. It wasn't officially on the market. I had never been in the place, but after looking at the 'numbers' I could see it was solid and had potential. Within a week we had arrived at a purchase price. We met at my attorney's office to make a cash payment.

When we left the closing, I decided it was time to go for a visit. I still had never been in the door. God put this in our path a decade before we needed it. I didn't even pay attention to the business because I was working on 'more important' operations (my perspective at the time). The franchise insisted that the owner be involved in the day-to-day operations. Vicki agreed to do it, and the rest is history. She didn't even take an income for ten years because we didn't need the money. In time, the ownership of the business was placed in Vicki's name.

Do you think God knew we would need that? Do you think God knew what He was doing, even when I was making other plans? I do. If that hadn't happened, we would have had no means to support Vicki during my time in prison. We would have lost our home. I can't imagine what she would have done to make a living. God provided seamlessly. He knew my brokenness was coming and prepared us for it.

What a beautiful truth. God is building on areas of my life that I don't even know about. My foundational premises, my values, and my mission for living are different than they have ever been.

I cannot live out a mission that praises God 'after the fact.' My mission must be completely owned, driven and commissioned by God and led by His Spirit. My definition of actionable belief must be re-written. What I am 'doing' must be secondary to what He is doing. No longer am I in charge of taking action. I am in daily pursuit of an intimate relationship with my Father, the God of all creation.

I trust what he is doing, even while I have been making other plans.

10-10-14 Journaling From Prison

Lord, I rejoice in your abundant supply. You are the resource and the solution. Help me to seek you in every situation, in the midst of my emptiness, weakness and brokenness. I have nothing and I can do nothing in the midst of the overwhelming needs of our circumstances, and I am in a place where even communicating about them is nearly impossible.

Together we are walking the path and I see the opportunities as you see them. You are the breath of life in every situation. Together, I press on knowing you are guiding; your grace is sufficient. There is opportunity in every situation. There is prayer in every breath as you imprint my life with your Spirit.

I have no ability to deal with future issues and I depend on you to do so. Finances, living arrangements, career, the joy of life... you are preparing the way before me. You protect and surround the family, and our unified prayers accomplish more than all of our plans and rehearsals ever did.

You open doors that no one can shut and your purpose is far beyond the momentary. Thank you. Let the eyes of faith shine in our hearts and illuminate our minds and perspectives in Christ Jesus.

My limits are the doorways through which you flow and use me. It's your presence and your plan, Lord, Amen.

Chapter Twenty-Three: Another Day Down

'Meaningless. Meaningless, says the teacher. Utterly meaningless. Everything is meaningless. What do people gain from all their labors... Generations come and generations go... What has been will be again, what has been done will be done again; there is nothing new under the sun.' (Ecclesiastes 1: 1-3a, 9 NIV)

There's an entirely new language spoken in prison. One of the most unique cultural phrases was the way time is defined. "How long have you been down?" I took a few laps around the nomenclature of that one. It seemed to express more than just time passing. It seemed to carry the connotation of a sub-culture, a sub-set of life that couldn't be considered actual living.

We were 'down.' We were paralyzed in time. Time passed only on the 'outside,' for everyone else. At the end of every day, inevitably you would hear someone say... 'Another day down.' The very purpose for a day became to get it "down" so we could be one day closer to living, to family, to freedom. Anything that would speed this day into the past was considered a good thing.

I worked as a young man with an older machinist. He entered the shop at 7am every day. The first words out of his mouth were, "Come on 4:30." It had become a joke, but in many ways it represents with accuracy the way we live our lives. Certainly, the future must be where our satisfaction resides.

Anyone past 30 has already begun to realize how quickly the days turn into years. (Let's face it: if you're my age, you really don't trust anyone under 30 anyway).

We are the sum of our experiences. Without a radical change in direction, each day we find ourselves further down the path we were already on. A little heavier and a little slower, eventually a little blurrier. We find that a pair of glasses in every room really isn't a bad idea. The trees we've planted (real or figurative) are taller than we imagined they could be. Our children are older than we feel *we* should be. Yet… we push on.

What choice do we have? Our routines are so 'routine' that if we happen to be driving on a familiar road, we might find ourselves at the office before we remember we were heading to Walmart.

We remember the fresh newness of our youth. Now, it appears as a faded merry-go-round. We see the young flexing their newfound place in the world. We sigh as we realize they are following the unseen, but endlessly repeated, cycles of all the generations before them. Their defiance or originality is only a mocking reminder to us. They too will soon know the agonies of life, the pain of normalcy and the yoke of meaningless expectations even Solomon could not escape.

I remind myself that every one of them has the 'right' to experience each step, just as I did, but I view it with cynicism as I already know their ending, even if they do not. Love fulfills them. Children fulfill them. A different husband or wife surely will fulfill them. A new job will fulfill them. Properly establishing blame on parents, a spouse, an employer, the church, the government, and even God, will ease their injustice. Money. Yes, money and more stuff will bring satisfaction. Power and influence. Status. Yes, those are the things they have been missing.

Where does it end? Where can it end as long as our trust is in ourselves and the skewed model of mentorship we have forged in self-defense? It ends in hate, in frustration, in anger, in discouragement and addiction. Sexual, substance, food, work, even addiction to distraction. How can we distract ourselves sufficiently, so that we will 'enjoy' our lives? It doesn't make sense and we know it. All we have accomplished is 'another day down.'

Everyone Has Advice

My past still vividly invades my thoughts. The top was spinning so fast I couldn't imagine how to change its direction. The building built so tall, how could the foundation be modified? Commitments had been made and the momentum of them was taking me where I had to go, whether I wanted to or not. Ever feel that way? Ever feel like the decisions were easy to make, but the fulfillment may take longer than you will live, or was that just me?

I don't want to insult you. I won't make some overall and trite observation. I remember how mad it made me when someone (typically someone who had no idea what it was like to run a business) tried to tell me...

- You shouldn't work so hard.

- You need to spend more time with your family.

- You should hire more people so you don't have to work so hard. (DUH, these employees are the reason I work so hard.)

- If you can't get it done in 40 hours, it doesn't need to be done.

- God will take care of the details, just trust Him more.

- Nobody, on their deathbed, ever wished they spent more time at the office.

I was especially angry when preachers ranted about workaholics, overtime and all of that. Don't get me started. My arrogance flared. I was responding to demands I was sure nobody in the entire world could respond to but me.

The things I *really believed* were fixed. I believed in God. I spent a lot of time talking about God, going to church and thanking God for blessing me. I didn't swear. I was a good guy. My premises looked something like this:

- God gave me talents and abilities that He expects *me* to use.

- Other people depend on me.

- My gift is making money. I give so others can minister.

- I am a decision maker and I have a gift for making decisions. Give me the information and I will make a decision.

- I am a negotiator and really good at it. I love making deals.

- Everything I work on is successful. God is blessing me. God likes what I am doing.

- I have responsibilities and I will do whatever it takes to fulfill those commitments.

No More Advisers, Please

I was the center of my life. Why not? My eyes are the only ones I see through. My perspective is the only one I have. People love me; they look to me for strength, for passion, for motivation, for decisions, for everything. They can't be wrong, not all of them. "God, bless what I am doing. Amen."

Some of the things I have shared I would never have said 'out loud.' These premises were different. I proclaimed them repeatedly and proudly. I really believed them. You may read them now and nod your head. I would have. In fact, this is the place in any book or conversation where I would have begun to pull back.

Oh yeah, here we go… another loser who's going to give me advice. I don't need *another* advisor. I don't need to hear a bunch of idealistic statements that have no way of being applied in my life. I am happy with my life and I am doing just fine.

Don't tell me how I should be doing it…

Look at me, I am already doing it.

Don't tell me how to be successful, I am already successful.

The blindness I faced was because I had not seen the other side. I had not imagined the destructive potential of the momentum I had created. I had not fathomed or factored in even the remote possibility that I could fail. In fact, it never even occurred to me with all of the money, all of the assets, all of the momentum and all of the accolades I had. It simply wasn't possible.

FASTER

Fear of failure requires pace, speed, and an ability to adapt and change. To live out the story of the Lion and the Gazelle. Whichever one you are, you know that when you wake up, you better be running.

Going fast was the only common theme of my life. I had a constant willingness to do whatever it took to win. As strange as it sounds, I don't ever want to lose that.

173

When I build with that drive on a poor foundation, it's just like the song goes: the foolish man built his house upon the sand and the rains came tumbling down. The house falls flat.

Was the house itself bad? Maybe not, but when I built on foundational premises that were egocentric, I built on sand. It defined the capacity for catastrophic momentum I would experience in my life. A fatal mistake. *Another day down.*

I confess, some of the things I've smoothed over about prison still stop my breathing. I have tried to humanize a situation which, at times, is far from human. I see prison experiences in God's Word and I wonder if they felt the same desperation; the heart-pounding 'get me outta here' moments that I felt. I wonder what their thoughts were as the hours of the night rolled on and they found no sleep.

'Another day down' has no purpose except to be 'down.' The circular logic of this is simple. The cascade of a day down is a path to the grave, not a path to fulfillment. Measuring life as we have always done results in getting what we have always received. Yet, we embrace this as 'normal' and we see brokenness as 'wrong.'

Is there really a difference in the furious emotion of our circular lives, whether in prison or free? Does purpose defined by shared human perspective have any more value than the prison reality which proclaims, 'another day down'? How long will time fill the ocean of our past before we acknowledge the wisdom that brought Solomon to his knees? … "Everything is meaningless."

'Another day down' does not stand between us and our life or our satisfaction. We don't have to wait. We are *not* in limbo. When we are the center of our lives, we rise and fall based on our own circumstances. We are completely dependent on them. We see massive distinction between our human perspective of strength and weakness.

The paradox of our faith is simply a notice given to all humankind that *every day* is just 'another day down.'

Like most of you, I prefer to read things written by people who 'weren't captured,' as Donald Trump recently said about John McCain (once a prisoner of war). I prefer to read about how people pulled themselves up by their own bootstraps; how they avoided the pitfalls and how I can avoid them too.

In brokenness, God showed me a pattern of cascading momentum. It has become my warning cry for family, friends and anyone who will listen. There is a cascade of brokenness. It exists. Only through God's eternal wisdom can we identify it and allow God to leverage it for His glory and our good. Once we embrace the fast and furious inversion of our thinking, we can begin to seek the paradox of Jesus Christ.

Let me share with you my thoughts on 'Transformational Brokenness.'

Chapter Twenty-Four: Transformational Brokenness

'Do not conform to the pattern of this world, but be transformed by the renewing of your mind. Then you will be able to test and approve what God's will is – his good, pleasing and perfect will.' (Romans 12: 2 NIV)

When you were a kid, did you ever throw a huge stone into a pond? Remember the gigantic splash? Nearly any size stone could make ripples, but the big ones were the most fun. Ripples would radiate immediately. Nothing you could do would stop the shockwaves until they bounced off the shoreline.

In many ways, this 'ripple effect' is a metaphor for my own story. For me, a single stone penetrated my life's surface the day the FBI raided my office. That moment, that stone, was just big enough to break through the surface of my complex system of beliefs.

Next came the ripple effect from the stone—the shockwave. Partners, friends, lenders, you name it, they were all affected. There was nothing I could do to stop it. The shockwaves of consequence spread without restraint. I was in the center, now motionless.

My own ripple effect made it seem as if an entirely new reality was being created within me, an alternate universe. This ripple effect had mesmerizing consistency. For every up there was now a down. For every past feeling of power, there was a future of helplessness.

I'd seen this ripple effect before, when things were out of control in an argument, but the stakes were smaller then. Even though I had noticed this ripple effect in my life before, I didn't realize I was the one causing it. How could a successful guy like me be the source of the ripples?

On the day I was sentenced to prison, my beliefs transformed into disbelief. Shockwaves. My disbelief transformed into brokenness. Here's the eye-opening news: my brokenness led to my transformation. How could being broken lead to transformation?

Sharing My Perspective

Here we are. You and I, sitting together as I share the stories of my life and hopefully convey the lessons I have learned from them. It all seems so clear to me. I lived them. I lived a life of self-deception and paid the price for it. It wasn't intentional, but the ripples continued long after I stopped paying attention. If we had talked a few years ago, the message would have been entirely different. I guess that's the point.

I had to go out early this morning and spend some time talking to God in the hot tub again. It would be so tempting to just share a bunch of stories with you and never really connect in a way that exposes the vulnerability of my life. It would be fun, but it would be reflective of the prideful man I used to be.

Do you think it's possible for the transparency of my life to overlay yours, perhaps just enough to make an intentional difference in your outcome? I hope so. Somehow I believe we face the same fears. We face the same desires for self-reliance and for the validation of others. Sure, I may have reached proportion that you can't imagine, but given time, the risk is there.

Can I help you avoid the trauma of being broken? Yes and no. You have your own 'ripple effect.' Let's face it, you've already experienced brokenness on some level. It has led you, in part, to this place in your life. But what did you do with that brokenness? Did you compartmentalize it or re-write it to conform within your memory? I thought so. We're more alike than you might care to think.

Writing this book is not about shock and awe, it is about you. It's about sharing the regeneration and transformation that are possible, even at the bottom. It's about sharing this with you.

There is one thing I am certain about: you're facing the same things I faced. Like me, you can't imagine what to do about it. The consequences of your actions seem paralyzing. What if I fail? What if I make the wrong choice? What if my family doesn't understand? Everyone is counting on you, and so you move on, doing what's expected and fracturing your purpose into manageable bites.

The Power of Cascading Momentum

There is something strange and powerful about momentum. You know, the 'ripple effect.' You've seen it at work, I'm guessing. It seems there is no end to the ways things can go wrong. When things go right, everything can just click into place. Suddenly you're taking credit for being a powerful and insightful leader. Momentum is a wonderful thing when it's on your side.

Have you ever thought about how to control momentum? Are you familiar with the idea of risk vs. reward? The more risk we take, the more reward we stand to gain. I lived by that concept for years. I learned to be very comfortable with taking risks. Finally, the momentum of those risks took me where I didn't want to go.

I believe there can be momentum and reward without risk.

Yes, you heard me. This is what I hope you take from all of our discussions: we control all of the variables that we can, but we simply can't control them all. We make decisions and commitments based on the understanding we have. We just don't have enough wisdom. But what if we did?

What would you do if you knew you could not fail? What would you decide today if you *knew* it would all work out for your good? What if you knew the path of hard work would leave you with a deep sense of peace and satisfaction?

You can.

"Martha, Martha," the Lord answered, "you are worried and upset about many things, but few things are needed—or indeed only one. Mary has chosen what is better, and it will not be taken away from her." (Luke 10: 41-42)

Yes, we think we are here to defend Him (I get that). Indulge me for a minute and think about the absolutely fantastic paradigm of God's relationship with us.

We don't know the future, but He does. We don't see how the decisions in life relate to each other and cascade into the future, but He does. If we really want to understand how powerful momentum can be in our lives, He is the one who created it. Even as the ripples on a pond radiate out from a single action, God is calling us to understand this principle of His creation. Our actions and reactions have momentum we cannot understand; sometimes we call those consequences. Likewise, the momentum God planned for your life can expand exponentially beyond your ability to ask or to imagine.

It's bigger than we are. Like any true belief, it defines our actions and our behavior. No matter what we *say* we believe, true belief dictates which side of momentum we find ourselves on. Transformational momentum reaches beyond fear or expectation.

You Don't Have to Climb Alone

I used to think being broken was a sad and horrible thing. It was painful, without question. It's hard to realize that decades of your life have been carried by the momentum of false beliefs. It's exhilarating to awaken to a life of enthusiasm that seems to gain momentum every day.

I was climbing a mountain. As I climbed, the air got thinner. People who were with me gradually fell away. The path got narrower. I left more things and people behind. They get the message. They leave you alone. It's lonely at the top.

Now I have found the momentum of God's path; the path that follows brokenness. Brokenness may be a paradigm shift more than anything else. Now it's time to break the grip of false and limiting beliefs, like releasing the flood gates that have been holding back water or breaking the chains of bondage that dictate our lives. The thrill of God's path reaches beyond brokenness.

The bible says the Spirit of God is like the wind: you can't see it, you can't tell where it came from or where it is going, but you know it's real. You've seen it's power. When you're traveling with it, your speed increases. Everything seems easier. You have momentum.

Momentum builds enthusiasm. More people are attracted to your journey. Your leadership and influence expand. You're no longer climbing into thinner atmosphere. You're gliding down the slope, celebrating as you cheer on your fellow climbers, even when it is hard work.

I don't create momentum, I participate in it. I can't manipulate it. I am so used to battling alone that I have to pinch myself at times. I'm not alone, you're not alone. Our brokenness is not a brokenness toward defeat. It is a brokenness that liberates.

Don't be afraid. God has you right where He wants you.

The momentum of transforming beliefs awaits you. It follows brokenness. Your death-grip on the ledge can be released. You can trust Him. Your brokenness will be the greatest ride of your life.

What Now?

You have a powerful tool in your hands. What will you do with it? For a brief moment, you have the clarity that can provide a tipping point in your life.

It's counterintuitive. Embracing brokenness doesn't sound fun. It may seem like the most risky thing you have ever done. Don't misunderstand. God's momentum doesn't preempt hard work. It doesn't mean you should shut off your brain. Everything you have experienced has been preparing you. Everything you have learned won't be forgotten.

It's a slight shift that makes a huge difference; the perfection of small things that bring massive results. Built on the cornerstone of Christ, the other foundation stones still include hard work and the drive of enthusiasm, but the momentum is key.

What will the ripple effect of your life be? What exchanges will you make in choosing it? Are you courageous enough to make the leap? Do you want to be the person you were created to become? I'm praying that God will show you. Even pain, suffering and prison are worth every moment. I don't want you to miss out on the thrill of the life you were meant for.

It's still a journey, you still make choices, you still face monsters. God's momentum is on your side. Keep allowing the bondage to be broken and nothing can hold you back.

I Was Created For This Moment

Today, I admit my fear that this book will not meet expectations. I surrender the lingering guilt that continues it's hammering in my subconscious from the past. I sense the presence of remaining barriers. They keep me from the lavish dimensions of oneness my Father God has for me.

My only hope lies in the continual process of being broken. Then I can remain free. The temptation to rebuild is too great. The automatic response systems are too well established. The natural tendencies of fear and doubt build shields without my permission.

I was created for this moment, to choose the momentum of transformational brokenness in my life. It is the paradigm of truth, the reward without the risk, renewal through brokenness.

Momentum is finally on our side.

5-19-15 Journaling From the Back Porch

I'm finally here. The endless night is over... or so it seems. The long nightmare. The furnace seven times hotter.

I wish I could say my prison sentence was unjust or righteous in some way. The idols of my own making were so clever I couldn't even see them myself, until they nearly destroyed me.

Nothing impedes Your divine WILL. Nothing truly defies You. You use it all, Lord, and it all conforms to Your purpose when it is complete. When I am complete, I will be the same: a glorious instrument for Your use, a vessel for Your filling, a being unlike anything I could have become on my own. A New Creature in Christ.

I want to remain broken in Your presence, Lord. Please remind me so I never again require Your intervention in such a dramatic way. Help me to remain broken before You.

My Broken Prayer

Dear God,

I am still looking off into the distance and weeping over the cascading effects of my failures. I can't turn back the clock. I can't change a thing I have done or how it has affected others. No amount of sorrow makes a difference. I don't know how to repair the damage or to redeem myself.

You are the only one who can redeem. You are the only one who takes broken pieces and uses them for good. I know You're doing that in me. Can You do that now in others who have been impacted by the cascade of my failures? Can You use the brokenness caused in their lives to bring them to Yourself? That is my prayer above all else, Lord God.

I can't make things right, but You can make things righteous by Your hand and Your purpose. Take my cascading brokenness and use it for Your glory.

Transform my brokenness into an instrument for good. Use me to channel Your endless renewal into a broken world which doesn't realize it is broken. Transform me into the man You created me to be.

I ask it all in Jesus' Name. Amen.

About the Author

Greg Yates is a Chicago area businessman writing from firsthand experience about extreme business success and failure. Greg's unique experiences in both corporate boardrooms and federal prison enable him to share the message of Christian businesses struggling with the implementation of timeless biblical principles.

Greg's humbling admission, *Broken*, is the testimonial foundation as Greg pursues the calling to awaken and equip Christian businessmen.

Is there a balance for Christians? How can we integrate ancient methodology into a process already moving at the speed of business? Is there really an actionable place for faith in my business? Can God really bring security when I don't have the answers? Are my struggles representative of a lack of faith, or the presence of sin in my life?

How can I get God on my timetable?

What is the *true purpose* of my life and my business?

Can God still use me after I have failed?

If you're engaged in the genuine struggle to honor God and survive in a world that almost never gets it right, download Greg's latest eBook for free: *Overcoming 10 Common Leadership FEARS: How to Turn Common Fear Into Your Uncommon Breakthrough.*

Greg writes and speaks to the Christian Business Leader who is willing to ask the most important questions about life and business.

As a Business Leader, you're on a journey and you don't need to go there alone.

You can follow Greg, his blog, podcast and future writing, at gregyates.net. Greg is also available for business events and seminars on a variety of topics, including his personal journey from wealth to prison and back to wholeness. For speaking engagements and all other inquiries, contact Greg at connect@gregyates.net.

Acknowledgements

I owe thanks to the following people for helping to make this book possible:

Vicki: Your love and belief in me has far exceeded my own. You've showed me how to depend on someone like I never imagined was possible. I love you with all my heart.

Terry: No father could be more proud or more inspired by their son. You've seen me at my best and worst. I want to finish well; to be the leader I should have been. To make you proud.

Laci: You deserve more than I could ever give. Your strength and resilience inspires me. You remind me of the joy in life and in family. You've always made me feel like a hero and I have clung to that through the darkness. When you're there, we're having fun.

Jim and Ruth: My biggest fans and most powerful prayer warriors. You planted the seed of faith in me and never doubted it would grow. You never gave up on me or lost sight of my destiny. The past is great, but the future is where your eyes have been and I have always found strength in that. Keep the coffee ready and my chair on your front porch available. I love it there.

Albert: You believed in an outcome of divine purpose in my life when I had given up. You never hesitated to speak it. Many avoided me but you never did. You were right: God had me right where He wanted me. Thanks for seeing past the failure.

Jaymie: The spark you gave me was vision for this book I didn't yet have. Your encouragement and strategic 'pushes' made this better. Nothing could repay you for the free gift of your belief. Thanks for sharing yourself and your time with this process.

Matt: You saw a framework for mission through my story when I couldn't. It's crazy how we were both prepared for synergy we are just learning to explore. Thanks for being a sold-out believer who sees business as a mission field. It's going to rock.

John: I couldn't have experienced breakthrough after brokenness if you hadn't pressed on through the barriers I threw up to stop you. I want to be a friend like you have been to me; to always believe that breakthrough is on the other side of resistance.

Bree: Your technical expertise and patient guidance (and red pen) made this book more enjoyable for the readers in ways I wouldn't have had the courage. Thanks for taking the time to question and understand my vantage point and passion. Everyone thanks you.

Finally, my Heavenly Father: Above all else, I am thankful for a loving and patient God who redeems all things and lets nothing be wasted. I am above all else humbled and blessed beyond my wildest dreams to be clay in the hands of an Almighty God.

Made in the USA
San Bernardino, CA
16 March 2017